Monetize Your Mindset

Create Financial Security
Monetize What
You Already Know

"If you don't find a way to make money while you sleep, you will work until you die."

~ Warren Buffett

Praise for *Monetize Your Mindset*

"Congrats, Bart, on this simple yet profound masterpiece that illuminates a revolutionary approach to creating and sustaining wealth. Monetize Your Mindset is a must read for everybody at every level of income because it is not a how-to-do book, it is a how-to-think book – a book that recalibrates the way we think about money, and how to make it."

~Dan Clark, New York Times Best Selling Author of *The Art of Significance*, Hall of Fame Speaker, University Professor.

Do you sometimes face financial hardship? For most, that's inevitable. How do you handle it? *Monetize Your Mindset,* is more than a how-to book; it fundamentally changes the way you think about money. It awakens your entrepreneurial spirit and helps you see opportunities all around you. Great for anyone trying to get ahead.

~ Ty Bennett, Author, *Partnership Is The New Leadership*

As a psychologist, I regularly counsel with my clients about the importance of mindset. *Monetize Your Mindset* takes the discussion to a whole 'nother level. Bart's straightforward approach to capitalizing on what we are already doing and what we are passionate about, makes a *lot* of sense. It also creates a sense of hope. Everyone has something to contribute, for which others will pay us. Usually it is much closer to us than we think. Bart illuminates the obvious through stories and examples that are clear, entertaining, and founded on solid psychological principles. Our mindset is worth more than we think!

~ Paul H. Jenkins, Ph.D., Positivity Psychologist

I am a mortgage broker. When the loan I am working closes, I am unemployed until the next deal comes my way. Creating a continuous stream of residual income excites me. *Monetize Your Mindset* stimulated my thoughts more than anything I've read in a long time. I am ready for the whole pie instead of a piece of someone else's pie! Great book! Thanks Bart!

~ Linda Creswell, Mortgage Loan Officer & Credit Repair Specialist

Monetize Your Mindset strikes a beautiful chord with me. For twenty years, I have made a great living just by utilizing my odd gift of a big mouth; singing and speaking, with funny voices and faces, telling stories... I am now encouraged to realize I can also create residual income from my unique talents. You can too! You'll find this an enlightening and engaging read. In fact, I had to force myself to stop reading when I was supposed to be working on something else! Love this book. It is a great read. Thank you Bart!

~ Jason Hewlett, CSP, CPAE, Hall of Fame speaker

I've been self-employed for over twenty years. I thought I had my bases covered, but this book has truly "monetized my mindset" inspiring many more ideas on how to create other revenue streams – a steady residual income along with my current business income. Thanks for motivating me, Bart.

~ Julie MacNeil, Financial Planner, Author, *The 50 Year Secret*

Would you like to create multiple streams of income by doing what you love? This book is a must-read! I have practiced the principles of this book in my own business. It changed the course of my life financially and emotionally in a way that truly makes the world a better place. Bravo to you, Bart. Thank you for letting me be a part of the journey.

~ Clint Pulver, Professional Speaker, "Be The Anomaly"

Dedication

This book is dedicated to my wife, Hiroko,
who puts up with my monetized mindset;
to my father who monetized my mindset;
and to Mom who motivated Dad to monetize.

Monetize Your Mindset

Make Money Fast with What You Already Have

Bart Merrell
Bart@BartMerrell.com
BartMerrell.com

Creative Editor: Thomas Cantrell
Tom@TomCantrell.com

Edit Team
Jenny Davis Staheli, Evelyn Jeffries, Su Boddie, Frank Lewis,
Dr. Paul Jenkins, Jesse B. Good, Rich Hopkins

Cover Design: Beth Dorfman Bearer

Photography: Ronald Ballok
RonaldBollok.com

Bart Merrell International Consulting Inc.
Copyright © 2018 by Bart Merrell All Rights Reserved
ISBN-13: 978-0692180600 (Bart Merrell)
ISBN-10: 0692180605

Table of Contents

"Money isn't everything – unless you don't have any (or you don't have enough)."

~ Bart Merrell

Chapter One ~
A Wake-up Call

What happens when what happens, happens? What happens when it happens to you? What will you do? What do you need to do? Can you afford to do it? What if you can't? What then?

What happens when what happens, happens, almost happened to my wife and me.

Hiroko, my wife, visits her family in Japan every year. She always has her annual health checkups while she's there.

During one such visit, she called from Nagoya, calmly informing me that initial tests indicated that she might have cancer. She made light of it. She jokingly said she needed to start looking for a new wife for me. She was so calm.

I was calm too – on the outside. On the inside – not so much. It was surreal. Maybe I didn't really believe it or accept the reality of it.

I began to research the information she had given me. As I focused on the reality of the situation, I felt a rising tide of panic and fear; fear that I might lose my wife, my best friend. This was not the first time I had ever felt this sense of fear and helplessness.

My only brother died of cancer when he was fifty-three. My sister died at age sixty-two, also from cancer. After the phone call from Nagoya, my mind began racing – leaping from possibilities to probabilities and back to possibilities – none of them good. I could lose my wife. I thought, "What am I going to do? We can't afford this."

Wait a minute. "We can't *afford* this?"

Why do my thoughts go to *money* so quickly? Money isn't everything, is it? Of course it isn't – unless you don't have any – or you don't have enough.

Money shouldn't have been a concern, but, sadly, it was. It wasn't that I didn't have any money. Financially, I was fine. It was that I didn't have the kind of resources that would see us through an extended fight with cancer.

I was suddenly afraid we didn't have enough money, certainly not enough for this kind of fight; not enough to deal with this – if it really happened. I simply couldn't drop everything and be by her side to support her – when whatever might happen, happens.

I felt helpless, inadequate – not enough.

They ran a series of tests. After eight sleepless nights, we received the results… The tumors were benign – negative for cancer. We were lucky. It was just a wake-up call.

A wake-up call is a call that startles you awake. It is usually frightening.

A wake-up call is also usually an opportunity. Sometimes it's even a chance for a do-over.

I'm now awake. Awake to possibilities of problems that I need to be prepared for. I'm also awake to possibilities, and the importance, of creating financial security for my family.

I realize that all of us should, could, need, to do the same thing for themselves and others we care about.

Hence, this book.

"Money isn't everything –
it's just right up there next to oxygen."

~ Zig Ziglar

Chapter Two ~
Money Isn't Everything...
...unless you don't have any!

Again, the question: What happens when what happens, happens?

What happens when you find yourself in the hospital; or your child or spouse is sick or injured and you need to be home to take care of them? Who pays your hospital bills? Your day-to-day expenses? House and car payments? Insurance premiums?

What happens when sick leave or family leave is used up? Most people's income stops. Will yours? What will happen to you, or to those you care about? How will you prepare for what happens before it happens? Because whatever happens certainly *will* happen.

It is imperative that you create or develop opportunities that give you multiple streams of income, residual income – a passive residual income. This goes beyond health insurance, which typically only pays the actual costs minus a deductible. The deductible *itself* can be financially crippling. You need something better than insurance. You need *assurance* – assurance of financial strength to battle what happens when whatever happens, happens.

Money isn't everything. True. In fact, by itself, money is nothing but paper and shiny metal. But what money *represents is* everything (or can enhance everything).

Money equals power, the power to overcome whatever needs to be overcome when what happens, happens. Money empowers you to help yourself, or others who need help, so that you don't end up standing by helpless when what happens, happens. Money isn't everything unless you don't have any or don't have enough. Not having enough money can mean the difference between life and death.

You have a job. You also have money in the bank – liquid assets that are immediately accessible. That's good. However, if you have to stop working for a period of time to heal, or to take care of yourself or someone else, you also need a steady residual income – hopefully some *passive* residual income – that comes to you every month.

Those eight days of sleepless panic following the bad news from my wife renewed my dedication to be financially strong enough to deal with whatever happens, *before it happens.*

When was *your* last "wake-up call"?

Do you really need a wake-up call that will scare the bejeebers out of you? How about not waiting for a wake-up call? How about just hearing me when I tell you to get ready *now*, so you are financially prepared to deal with whatever happens before it happens – because it certainly will happen.

Fellow speaker and author, Douglas Nelson, was severely burned from the waist up in a home accident. He was airlifted to the university hospital in Salt Lake City, Utah He said, "I spent six weeks in a coma… [then] nine months of agonizing slow, painful, rehab, learning how to do all the little things each of us takes for granted: talking, eating walking… literally learning how to be comfortable in my own skin."

He had to focus on survival and on healing. He was fortunate. He could afford to do that. Others could not.

Doug had multiple streams of passive residual income that came to him whether he worked or not. He did not have to worry about money. All he had to do was get well.

It was not the same for others in the burn unit. Most patients worried about finances. They could not focus on just getting well; they had to keep things together financially while they got better. This kind of worry and stress did not help them heal.

Most of them, however, did have one thing to be grateful for. Their families and friends could, would, and did, visit to offer their support.

One little boy, however, did not have even that much relief. No one came to see him – no family, no friends – nobody, not even his mother.

This eighteen-month old had accidently fallen into a camp fire. He was taken to the burn unit and left there to heal without the comfort and presence of his mother. The hospital, with its hollow corridors and the constant clicking, humming, hissing, thumping – the around the clock sounds of pain and survival – created a frightening, alien place for a little boy.

It would be scary and painful for *anyone,* but a young child in so much pain and all alone? Can you imagine his bewilderment and agony? This was a life-threatening situation, and especially traumatic for someone so young.

Of course the nurses did what they could, but they were not family. They were not his mother. She could not afford to miss work, nor could she handle the cost of travel to come visit her little boy. She had to stay home and earn money to pay bills so the child would have a home and a family to come back to when he got better.

Can you imagine being forced to choose between giving up your job so you can be with your child during his time of crisis, or keeping your job and paying the bills so he or she would have a home and a family to come back to?

This story is recounted in Doug Nelson's book, *Catch Fire: How To Ignite Your Economy,* Doug says, "Wow, what a terrible decision for a parent to have to make."

What would you do? What *could* you do?

Financial preparedness is a must. You never know what will happen until it happens; but you *do* know how much easier life will be when you have the resources to battle whatever happens when it happens.

This is more than just dealing with disaster, however. This has to do with enjoying a higher standard of living, a much better place to *exist.*

Ordering off the Left Side of the Menu

When I was twelve years old, I was sitting with my family in a dinner theater in Durango, Colorado. My Uncle Webb was an actor in the play. He sat with us for a few minutes before the play started and told us we could order anything on the menu. We could have whatever we'd like.

Wow! I can get anything I want? Cool!

I deliberately chose the most expensive thing on the menu: prime rib. I had never had prime rib before but it must be good; it was the most expensive thing listed.

My dad was well off financially, but he was quite conservative, and his kid just ordered the most expensive thing on the menu.

"No, Bart! You don't need that."

Uncle Webb insisted, "It's fine; he can order whatever he wants. It's on the house."

So I got prime rib (I've had a love affair with prime rib ever since).

It was a remarkable experience – not just the dinner itself, but being able to order off the left side of the menu for the first time in my young life.

What does it mean to "order off the left side of the menu"? Well...

What is on the left side of the menu? What you want – the details, the description.

What is on the right side of the menu? The price – the financial cost to you.

The ability to order off the left side of the menu means you get what you want or need *without* being overly concerned about what is on the right side of the menu – the price.

That is how financial security feels. It is more than just being able to deal with what happens when what happens, happens; it is establishing an enhanced standard of living.

How do you position yourself to gain that financial security? *Monetize Your Mindset.*

"It had long since come to my attention that people of accomplishment rarely sat back and let things happen to them. They went out and happened to things."

~ Leonardo da Vinci

Chapter Three ~
Monetize Your Skillset

What do you *like* to do? What do you *need* to do? What are you *already* doing? How could you make money doing *that*?

The way to be prepared to deal financially with whatever happens, whenever it happens, as Doug Nelson was able to do, is to monetize.

Monetize your skills, your abilities, your talents, your experience, and even more important, *Monetize Your Mindset*, so you are automatically looking for ways to make money by doing what you like to do, need to do, or are already doing.

This will help you create the kind of income Doug had – a steady, dependable income that allowed him to focus on healing. Create the kind and level of income that will allow you to focus on your loved ones in their time of crisis and healing, if a crisis happens.

Am I telling you anything you don't already know? If you are working, you already have naturally monetized skills and skillsets, and you may be profiting from them – at least to some extent – but until now, you've likely never thought about it, or the process of doing it.

You have undoubtedly never thought about monetizing your mindset.

When you were young, did you learn to do something at home, then later do it for someone else for pay? For example, did you learn to care for your little brother or sister? Then did Mom and Dad start paying you to take care of your younger siblings while they went out? Did you subsequently get hired to babysit for friends or neighbors? That is a simple example of monetizing a skill set (child care). You are offering your skills to an employer for a wage, usually an hourly wage. It is a natural process. Traditionally, though certainly not exclusively, girls would baby sit and boys would do yardwork, a skill they too learned at home, which they then marketed to friends and neighbors. This is Level One monetization.

Let's take it to the next level. After having some experience with monetizing the skillset of taking care of your siblings, and later the children of neighbors and friends, perhaps you found that you enjoyed that kind of work, or were at least good at it. You might then have started a business that eventually evolved into an enterprise, such as a preschool or daycare.

Or perhaps you became so good at yard care that eventually you opened a landscaping business. When you began to work for someone else for pay, it is the *first* level of monetizing a skillset.

When you began to work for yourself, rather than an employer, you are at Level Two of monetizing a skillset. You are still monetizing skillsets, but you are working for yourself, not an employer. You have, in effect, cut out the middleman, and are serving clients directly.

We acquire these skills at home, or working for others, or in school, or they come to us naturally.

When you learn how to do something at a trade school or university (accounting, say, or brain surgery), then go to work for someone else – an employer – doing the thing you've learned how to do, and getting paid for it. you've monetized a skill or a skillset.

When you learn a skill and realize you could sell it or make money doing it, and go into business for yourself doing it, you've monetized a skillset.

Both these pathways are monetizing something you like to do, need to do, or are already doing anyway.

Monetizing your mindset is the *third* level of thinking. It involves both the first two levels, and it's an expansion of the concept. When you have a monetized mindset, you are constantly thinking of all the things you do that you could monetize. Things you like to do, things you need to do, and things you are already doing.

So, in summary…

Level One ~ Monetize your skillsets – and go to work for someone. For example, you attend medical school, graduate, and then go to work for someone else.
When you get a job and get paid for it, as most people do, you are actually monetizing a skill or a set of skills. You learn skills and put them to work for someone else and, in return, you get a small (sometimes miniscule) piece of the action. You can further monetize things you do well on your job by customizing, specializing, or getting a better assignment or promotion, but you are still working for someone else and getting a relatively small share of the results.

Level Two ~ Monetize skillsets – and go to work for yourself. You develop talents, skillsets, and interests and monetize them, profiting from them outside formal employment. For example, you go to medical school then temporarily work for someone else while you gain experience and hone your medical skills, eventually opening your own practice.

Level Two is not about figuring out how to get an extra job working for someone else. That's still Level One thinking. Level Two thinking is about finding clients and customers, not employers.

This level could also include signing up to sell someone else's product or service, such as joining an affiliate or network marketing program, or purchasing a franchise. In any case, you are independent to the extent that you don't have to answer to an employer.

Level Two is doing something on your own that creates a greater income. It might be a small supplemental income, or it could be (or could become) a significant income, and ultimately take the place of your traditional "real job." However, even if you develop an international reputation, such as Dr. Seuss or J.K. Rowling and become rich and famous, you are still just monetizing a skill or a skillset, and that is still Level Two.

Remember, Level One is working one or more jobs – for someone else. It may be a day job or night job, full or part time, or any combination. Level Two is working outside your day job. You are working for yourself. You are self-employed. This is the beginning of the entrepreneurial mindset. You are getting a bigger piece of the pie you, yourself, baked, but you are still working a "job."

Now you are ready to consider ...

Level Three ~ *Monetize Your Mindset.* Monetizing your mindset is related to Levels One and Two, but it is much more than monetizing (getting paid for) individual skills or even skillsets.

Monetizing your *mindset* is fundamentally altering the way you look at things. You are always considering:

What do I *like* to do?
What do I *need* to do?
What am I *already* doing?

How can I monetize it?

"You were put on this earth to achieve your greatest self, to live out your purpose, and to do it courageously."

~ Steve Maraboli

Chapter Four ~
Monetize your Mindset

Several years ago I decided… well, actually, my *wife* decided, that I had been working on my "before" picture long enough. It was now time to start working on my "after" picture. It was time for me to lose some weight.

It's a common phenomenon that before we get married we are inspired to look our best. Then something happens.

Before I got married, I was looking pretty good. My weight was in check and I was in decent shape. Then I got married. In some mysterious way, fifty pounds was packed onto my six foot, four inch, frame. Now, I'm not blaming my wife for my weight gain, but it did seem to coincide with our marriage and her good cooking.

I'm a pretty tall guy, so that wasn't a horrible amount, at least that is what I told myself, but it wasn't pleasing either, to either of us. Hiroko wanted me to look like I did the day we were married. In order to do that, I needed to lose about fifty pounds.

"Getting back to my wedding weight" is a typical goal for married people who decide they want to lose weight.

Hiroko and I are very open with each other, and also gentle. That's a unique combination. We joke about everything. By the time she gently joked that she'd really like to see less of me, I already knew what she meant.

It was time. I had to find a way to get back to my wedding weight. In that same moment, my monetized mindset kicked in. *If I am going to lose weight, I am going to get paid to do it.*

Marie Osmond did it. So did Dan Marino. They used a weight loss program that worked for them, *and they got paid for sharing it with others.*

They became spokespersons for Nutrisystem®. They monetized something they needed to do – lose weight.

The moment I got serious about losing the weight, I automatically started brainstorming a good domain name that would attract people to the hoped-for solution for my weight problem.

BackToMyWeddingWeight.com sounded good. A quick search on Godaddy.com told me it was available, so I bought it.

But wait, I hadn't even found a system that worked. So why did I purchase the domain name? Because I knew that sooner or later, I would *find* a system that worked for me and, because of my mindset, I also knew I'd find a way to get paid for helping other people solve the problem I was setting out to solve for myself. (If Marie Osmond could do it, so could I.)

An essential element of monetizing your mindset is being prepared to take advantage of any opportunity when it comes along. Opportunities show up all the time, but they don't always translate instantly into an income.

It took me eight long and frustrating years to find a system, a process that worked – for me and, of course, for others. Nevertheless, I got prepared long before that, starting with purchasing an appropriate domain name as soon as I began my search for something that would actually work.

It seemed to me that every weight loss program available was less about the product and more about the ninety-day challenge of working my butt off (literally) in the gym – while starving myself to death.

The reason I say "ninety-day challenge" is because every "system" I tried was a "ninety-day challenge." Well, of course, if you go the gym regularly and eat less for ninety days, you will lose weight. You might not *keep* if off, but you *will* lose it.

Going to the gym and starving, however, is not in my DNA. Like most people, I have just enough willpower to get to the gym that first day, pay for a three-year membership, and never go back again.

You've been there, haven't you? C'mon, admit it!

My dear wife patiently put up with my noble efforts and loved me anyway. Then one day I had a "Eureka!" moment.

After years of searching, I finally found a system. It included a product that actually worked. It was not about a ninety-day challenge of me getting my butt to the gym and dieting for ninety days. All it required was to focus ten days at a time. In two months and five days, I demolished forty-eight pounds, and I was back to my wedding weight – without ever having to get my lazy butt to the gym.

Here's the point. You don't have to be passionate about everything you do to make money. In fact, it doesn't have to be something you *want* to do at all. I am *not passionate* about weight loss. Weight loss was not something I *wanted* to do; it was something I *needed* to do. And if I was going to do it anyway, why not get *paid* to do it?

My habit of monetizing was so ingrained in my thinking (mindset) that, as I said, I bought the domain years before I actually used it. Now BackToMyWeddingWeight.com is the source of another stream of income; again, not because I'm passionate about weight loss, or even enjoy it, *but because I needed to do it and was going to do it anyway.* So I figured out a way to make money while helping others with a similar challenge.

Monetizing your mindset tends to create a much larger income than just monetizing skills or skillsets one at a time. In Level One you are getting a small piece of someone else's pie. In Level Two you are getting a larger piece of your own pie. But in Level Three you are getting a larger piece of *your own* pie and likely pieces of many other pies.

Monetizing your Mindset is a way of looking at the world. It is the entrepreneurial way of seeing things. It's about noticing everything you do for yourself and for others and wondering if, and how, it could become a source of income, particularly residual or passive income, or both.

Some are things you are passionate about; some are things you have to do; and some are things you are already doing anyway, or someone else is, and you can make money from piggybacking onto their efforts or joining with them in their business. So… why not?

Many of the things you can monetize are items, ideas, or programs that someone else is doing or has invented, and you obtain the rights to market them or purchase them for resale.

It is this mindset that caused me to automatically consider how I might make money from losing weight before I ever even figured out *how* I was going to actually lose weight.

It is a habit of thinking, a way of looking at things, an attitude, if you will. An attitude is a position you take toward the things you do whether or not you are passionate about them – or even if, frankly, you don't particularly enjoy them – like losing weight; but you *do* enjoy the process of helping others and making money in the process. Obviously it gets even better when the things that you do are things you enjoy and, better yet, are passionate about.

So, how do you create a monetized mindset? It's not that complicated, really. It's a mental adjustment, a broader focus, a habit of thinking that drives your action. It is an awareness; being aware of possibilities – the opportunities that are all around you.

Monetizing your mindset is essentially training a new response to something you do for yourself that worked for you, something that solved a problem, or something you simply enjoyed doing. The old response was, "That was great!" The new response is, "That was great! Now how might I share it with others and get paid for doing it?"

This is obviously more profitable than following your normal, untrained reflex reaction: "Cool! That worked. It solved my problem (or it was fun)," and then moving on. That is what we normally do, and we move on without seeing the possibilities for profit in the experience.

When you start to automatically consider what you could do to provide the service or product you used for yourself to help others with the same problems, and, in the process, figure out how to get paid for your efforts, you have developed a monetized mindset.

There is no need to do stuff that you don't want to do. Many people have one or two part-time jobs in order to make ends meet. I feel like yelling, "Stop it!" Stop working yourself to death in dead-end, part-time jobs, especially doing things you don't like to do. Stop wasting your life doing jobs that give you such small ROI (return on investment – of time).

Not only do they give you a small return on your time investment, they may take more from you and your family than the financial return could ever be worth.

These jobs have potentially a huge downside. At a drug rehab center where I volunteer, I hear many stories about abuse and neglect. There is one story that stands out. It is not, however, about abusive parents. It is about parents that were not available. They weren't bad parents; they were just trying to provide for the family.

Edwin was telling his story of being sent to prison at age fifteen. He's now twenty-nine and, in the past fourteen years, has only spent five months outside of prison. He tells it this way:

"My parents weren't bad parents. They just weren't there. They both had at least two jobs at any given time. I remember walking home alone from school – rain, snow, or shine in elementary school. I watched other kids get picked up by their parents. I always wished someone would pick me up, especially when it rained or snowed, and take me home. It never happened."

"I ended up in a gang at age eleven. Why a gang? Because they were there for me. They felt like family to me. They took care of me. In exchange, I had to do things that I knew were wrong. The gang experience led down a path that got me hooked on drugs and eventually incarcerated – for a long time."

Edwin's parents did the best they knew how. I don't know them personally, but surely it is possible that if they had created a monetized mindset, they would have been able to invest their time differently and been around more for Edwin.

We live in a time when there are an infinite number of ways to create multiple streams of income. The internet is a marvelous tool for getting your message out, building an audience, marketing and promoting your idea, your product, your service, or products or services you've used and want to promote.

Using the internet, you can monetize nearly anything you like to do, need to do, or are already doing. Do you like quilting? Start a quilting blog and build a following. Give your readers good information. Create a product or service related to quilting and market it. Alternatively, market someone *else's* product or services on your blog or website. Write a book about quilting and promote it. Speak about your topic (whatever it is) at organizations, and sell your book from the back table. As you get more proficient at presenting, you build a site that promotes you as a consultant or trainer and speaker, and get paid for speaking. You don't have to have a "big stage" or "rock star" personality to do this. There are many organizations that would love to have you speak about what you are promoting, or about the process you went through to turn a hobby into an income-producing activity. When you get relatively good at it, they will pay you to speak – creating another source of income.

Every time (practically speaking) someone with a monetized mindset does almost anything, they at least cursorily think "How can I monetize this so that whether it is something I like to do, need to do, or am already doing it will pay for itself. More importantly, it will produce an income, a long-term, residual, hopefully passive, income.

Don't ask: "Can I monetize this?"

Ask: *"How* can I monetize this?

Most of the time you spend monetizing successfully is in deciding *what* you will monetize and how you will make it work for others, not just yourself – especially when you wish to make a real difference and are not satisfied to just provide junk products and services. Monetizing your mindset is getting your brain conditioned to think constantly how to monetize anything and everything. Of course you won't monetize everything you think about. You do, however, constantly and automatically, think about the *possibility.*

Creating a monetized mindset is an important mental adjustment. It creates the habitual mental perspectives that help us create residual income, for which there is a real need.

There are different definitions out there for "residual income" but, for the purpose of this book, residual income is when you continue to get paid after the work is done. Residual income includes such things as royalties from books, movies, or songs; income from real estate or business investments; a flow of income where you don't actually have to be present to earn it.

The need for such an income is growing, not diminishing. After all, we are residual spenders. Your mortgage or rent, your food and utilities, and many other bills you have to pay accrue twenty-four hours a day, seven days a week.

So what is the process? How do we create or develop a monetized mindset so we accrue income twenty-four-seven?

First, consider how a monetized mind thinks. When someone with a monetized mindset creates, builds, purchases, or does something to solve a problem or fill a need – or have fun – they tend to think, "How can I monetize this?"

Whether it is something they like to do, need to do, or are already doing for themselves, their boss, or co-workers, the monetized mindset thinks constantly, habitually, automatically about ways that activity could pay for itself. More importantly, how it could produce an income – a long-term residual, hopefully passive, income.

Residual income comes in every month but requires some kind of activity to maintain it. Passive income comes in every month with little to no activity needed to maintain it. The less activity that is needed, the more passive the income is.

Monetized minds don't just think, "*Can I* monetize this?" They think, "*How will I* monetize this?" Then they try it. Sometimes it works, sometimes it doesn't. Sometimes it works really well. Gary Vaynerchuk, in his book *Crushing It*, says, "You are better off being wrong ten times and right three times than you are if you only try three times and you always get it right." Why? Because you learn something even when you fail.

When did the idea for this book, *Monetize Your Mindset*, really click with me? When I was listening to a speech given by a resident at the drug rehabilitation center I mentioned earlier. It was her first speech at the Toastmasters club that I helped lead. As she spoke about her upbringing, the abuse and neglect she suffered at home – she emphasized that it only happened at home. When they were out and about, everyone acted normal. Everyone was sober, or close to sober. They were reasonably kind – not overtly abusive. She assumed all families were like that, one way at home, another in public.

Her exact words were, "I thought my life was normal. Until I went to college, I thought that everyone else's lives were the same as mine."

My own experience was different. I had two parents who loved and encouraged me and my siblings. I thought *that* was normal. (I've since found out that it isn't normal and just how lucky I am.)

It really hit home during her speech. The way people *think* about money and opportunity is formed by the experiences they had growing up. The way their parents thought about money creates the family mindset about money and creates their children's money mindset blueprint.

If you did not grow up with my dad or someone like my dad, then you likely don't have a monetized mindset. But that's okay, I'll help you develop one, and it will be fun!

That's why I wrote this book – and why I make the training and personal consultation offer – to help you *Monetize Your Mindset*; to help you advance your thinking so you start noticing the hundreds of opportunities that are right under your nose.

Stop living paycheck-to-paycheck. A major car problem or health issue can throw you into financial disaster and personal despair. *Monetize Your Mindset*, and build multiple streams of residual income – checks that come in whether or not you can work your regular job. That is financial security.

That is what this is all about. That is what this book is for. That is what my coaching is for. To create a monetized mindset so you achieve financial security; so you are prepared to deal with whatever happens when what happens, happens, and live a life of peace and security.

"Success is knowing your purpose in life, growing to reach your maximum potential, and sowing seeds that benefit others."

~ John C. Maxwell

Chapter Five ~
What Can You Monetize?

Can anyone do this? Can anyone monetize skills and skillsets? Can anyone develop a monetized *mindset?* Yes. It's really just getting in the habit of asking yourself these simple questions:

"What do I *like* to do? What do I *need* to do? What am I *already* doing? How can I monetize it?"

When you find these questions rolling around in your head, you have the mindset. Then it's on to the next level: *Do it!* Try it. Take a chance. See if it works … It's not that complex of an idea.

Money from Honey

My friend, Brad Barton, had wondered about beekeeping for some time. It seemed like something he could do. Others had done it, so, why not him? His kids might even like it, who knows?

One day, on his way home after a speech with his presentation coach (Brad is a professional speaker), he decided to take a look at some beekeeping equipment and supplies. He pulled into a nearby beekeeping supply shop, looked around for a bit asked some pointed questions, and left the shop with the beginnings of a beekeeper's business.

Actually, in his mind, it was not really a business – at this point he thought of it as just a hobby (the difference between a hobby and a business is that hobbies *cost* money, businesses *make* money. If your business is costing you money, then maybe you should consider it an expensive hobby – and decide if it's worth it!).

Brad started beekeeping just for fun and for ten years he did just that – had fun. He kept bees. He made honey – but not money – until a friend (who, ironically, Brad had helped get started beekeeping) said something to this effect: "Brad you could do this another way. You can make money at this." He showed Brad his system of marketing the honey his hives produced, marketing the services his bees provided (pollinating fields and orchards), creating starter kits (hive nuclei), etc. and making a profit from his hobby.

The light bulb turned on in Brad's head. Central to his keynote speech's inspirational theme to challenge his audiences to do something they've never done – maybe something no one has ever done. Keeping bees was something Brad had never done. Then it was something he'd never made money at. Now he does.

Today, he and his kids make somewhere between fifteen to twenty thousand dollars a year in extra income because he monetized something that was once a fun hobby (and is still a fun business).

When you *Monetize Your Mindset*, you can indeed make *Money from Honey.*

Cash in on Conflict

How about monetizing conflict? Prize fighters, mercenary soldiers, and lawyers are not the only ones who do that. It's often said, "When life hands you lemons, you make lemonade."[1] Okay, then, as long as you are making lemonade for yourself, set up a lemonade stand and make money making lemonade for others.

Many years ago, my friend, Thomas Cantrell, was the Human Resources Director for a Native American tribal government. One day an employee of the finance department

---

[1]   Elbert Hubbard in a 1915 obituary penned and published for actor Marshall Pinckney Wilder.

came to his office, told him she had been fired, and asked if she could appeal the termination of her employment.

He assured her that the rules allowed for that, then asked her why she had been fired (the matter hadn't yet officially reached his desk). Her reply was interesting.

She said, "I probably deserve to be fired, I was late a lot."

Native Americans, particularly in that tribe, were rarely on time – for anything. The clock simply wasn't important in their culture. If they said they'd do something, they generally did it, but they didn't march to the tune of a ticking time clock. (We should take a lesson – we might live longer!)

Thomas asked the employee if she had been warned and given a chance to improve. She acknowledged that she had, and said again that she felt she likely deserved to be fired, but she still wanted her hearing. She didn't actually call it a "hearing," she called it her "speak."

"I want my speak," she said.

It seemed odd to him. She wanted to be heard, but didn't seem to have a much of a case, and didn't want her job back or damages or anything. Why did she want to be heard? And why did she call it her "speak"? What was going on?

Perplexed, Thomas notified the employee's boss of her request. Rather than respond with the usual acknowledgment of her right to be heard, the head of the finance department where the employee had worked came immediately to my friend's office.

He was obviously stressed, nervous. He first requested, then demanded, that the employee's right to be heard be denied. Thomas wondered what she had to say that the department head didn't want said.

Thomas explained to the department head that while he understood that the employee's request did seem odd, the tribal policy was clear; her right to be heard was not conditional on the strength of her case, or even any reasonable request for remedy. The policy simply said that any tribal member who was disciplined for any reason could have a hearing before the Personnel Review Board (made up entirely of tribal members) if they so desired, even if that employee admitted they were wrong.

It made sense in the context of tribal culture. The tribe had a tradition of everyone having their right to their "speak." Perhaps that was the foundation of the policy. At tribal gatherings every tribal member, regardless of age or social status, had the right to stand and talk, about anything, for as long as they wanted to speak. They didn't have to make a point. In fact, their stories usually didn't have a point, a moral, or any kind of punch line. They were just stories, narratives. They could, and did, talk about anything.

It was their daily news or weekly blog, so to speak. This tribe didn't have a written language. Speaking about anything and everything that interested them or affected their daily lives, whether it seemed "important" or not, was part of the fabric of their culture: it was an early form of social media.

Thomas reminded the department head of this policy and the probable reasons behind it, but the department head pushed back (he was not Native American). He tried to bribe my friend to deny his employee's right to be heard. He said that because he controlled the tribe's finances, he had been able to stash hundreds of thousands of dollars away in places that even tribal officials didn't know about and would give Thomas any kind of budget he wanted.

"You want another secretary? Better office equipment? You want an increased salary?" He said he'd fund any project, any position, any budget request. When my friend reminded him that this sounded very much like bribery, and bribery of a tribal official was illegal, the department head stormed out of his office and soon instigated a full-on attack to discredit the HR Director and get rid of him.

His tactics worked. Thomas was fired. The tribal member did not get her hearing, her "speak."

Thomas is not one to take this kind of thing lying down. He appealed his case. He won. The opposition pushed back. My friend won again. This was not fun, but at least he was winning. They pushed back a third time. My friend won a third time.

This was starting to get… well… not exactly fun… but it was interesting.

They pushed back a fourth and fifth time. Thomas won again and again. Six times they fought him. Six times he won.

He thought, "Hey, I'm good at this!" It wasn't something he wanted to do; it was something he had to do anyway, and in the process Thomas found out he was pretty dang good at it.

One day, he went on a blind date. During the course of getting to know each other, his date said that she had lost her job, and it wasn't fair. Thomas represented her just to help her out of a tough situation (in this particular area of administrative law, a human resources professional can represent a client without having to be an attorney at law).

He won her case. She asked how much she should pay him. He had no idea. He hadn't thought of charging her; he was just helping her through a tough situation, similar to the one he had faced. She insisted on paying him a percentage of the amount she was awarded.

He accepted. She paid him by tying twenty dollar bills to the branches of a small money tree (a branch stuck in a tin can). As he gazed at the money tree, it dawned on him that he could do this. He could help others with his new-found skill and get paid for it.

So he did. He monetized conflict.

He took out a yellow page ad listing his personal phone number. Instead of renting an office, he met clients at their local library. His company, Utah Advocates, evolved into National Administrative Law Advocates and is now Administrative Trial Advocates, International. Over four decades later, he is still representing people in this specialized area of administrative law and getting paid for it.

Thomas monetized employment conflict – something that he didn't particularly enjoy but had to deal with anyway. He realized he was good at it – and it became fun. Soon, administrative trial advocacy and conflict resolution became his core profession. Over four decades later, he is still in the business. He has a documented 97% win rate in the administrative courts and is having a lot of fun making a positive difference in hundreds of people's lives by empowering them to win.

He also speaks professionally about professional, personal and political conflict resolution and transforming conflict into connection and creative, constructive, collaboration. He gets paid for that too.

If you ask him, Thomas will tell you that he does nothing professionally today that he didn't once do for free, just for fun, or just because he had to. It took a friend who insisted on paying him for helping her to get him to realize that he could monetize something he was good at, whether he initially enjoyed doing it or not.

What are you doing that maybe you don't particularly enjoy doing, but you have to do anyway? Have you gotten good at it? Do you think it could be something you could enjoy helping others do? If so, how about monetizing it? Like my friend, Bob Kittell did. He monetized memory.

Monetize Memory

Bob was not enjoying his college experience. His grades were okay, but it was a struggle.

There was something Bob had to do to graduate. Get decent grades. There was something Bob had to do to get decent grades. Remember stuff. Facts, figures, names, dates, formulas, names of rocks, names of species…

Bob wasn't very smart. Actually, he was smart, but like millions of others, especially students who were intimidated by the rigors of college, he *thought* he wasn't very smart. He had a lousy memory. Actually, he had an excellent memory, but like millions of other students, he *thought* he had a lousy memory.

He was mistaken on both counts. He *was* smart. He had a great brain; he just didn't realize it. He had an excellent memory; he just had to learn how to use it.

One day a friend suggested that he look up a certain book about memory improvement. He thumbed through it and then realized, "Hey, I could do this!" And he did.

He studied the techniques and learned how to more effectively and easily access his computer brain. He learned how the brain stores information and how it recalls it – just like the computer this book is being written on. He learned how to easily and simply remember (store and recall) a whole lot of important information. He found out he was a heck of a lot smarter than he had realized.

He knew that other students, thousands of them, were having the same issues at school that he had been having. He realized that many, like him, felt they were not very smart; that they were not good students, and were struggling.

He also knew that many who *did* know they were smart and *did* get good grades were working a lot harder and spending a lot more time studying than was necessary, just because they didn't know how to use their computer brain in the way it was designed to be used.

When human beings discover something of value our instinct is not to hoard it and keep it to ourselves. No, humans are, by nature, social creatures. Our human instinct is, to share our discoveries with others – anybody, everybody, neighbors, strangers, friends, family.

So Bob started showing his friends what he had learned. They tried it. It worked! They started doing better – much better – on their tests.

The best part about it all was they were having fun – and Bob was having a blast helping them have fun! He conducted seminars all over campus. He helped groups of students blow the curve in their respective courses. Professors started wondering, "What happened to Dumb Bob and where th' heck did Smart Bob come from?"

He leaned into this new found-mission, enhancing what he had learned, developing special approaches for specific courses. Bob had already graduated – but here he was, still on campus, helping other students learn what he wished he could have known while he was struggling to get his modest "B" average.

What a thrill to help students he had once looked up to! He helped medical students with pathology and pharmacology. He helped law students gain an exquisite command of case law. He helped Master's students writing their thesis and preparing for their oral exams. He helped Ph.D. candidates defend their dissertations.

As I said, Bob had graduated and was still living in his college town, but was not planning on returning to school. Two of his former university professors told him he should. He should get his Master's degree – perhaps in communications. Based on what he was doing, they thought he would be an excellent teacher or trainer.

Bob hadn't thought of that. He had spent uncountable hours in the library to barely pull off a 3.0 GPA and earn his Bachelor's degree. He'd had enough. It was exhaustingly hard work, and he had made up his mind to never go back. In the meantime (ironically, after he had graduated), he had learned the memory techniques and was sharing them all over the campus where he had been a student. He hadn't put two and two together. He didn't hate school; he hated the frustration and hard work.

He realized his distaste for school was based on the mind-set of "Dumb Bob." With new-found enthusiasm for learning, and confidence born of his memory techniques, "Smart Bob" decided to give it a go. He enrolled in the Master's program.

The acid test of Bob's new improved brain was a challenging communications class. Before giving the group their first test, the professor informed them that in sixteen years, no one had ever achieved a perfect score on any of his fifty-question multiple choice tests.

Bob not only earned a perfect score on that first test – he did it in twenty-seven minutes.

His professor felt that Bob must have cheated. "There's no way you could get a perfect score – especially in such a short period of time." He said that the average time to take the test was an hour – not less than a half an hour – and the highest score closest to Bob's was in the 80s. Ergo, Bob must have cheated.

Bob pushed back. "Just for fun, why don't you ask me anything from the four chapters we were just tested on?"

The professor grabbed his book.

Bob thought, "Wait! He wrote the book, so why does he have to refer to it?"

The professor opened it at random, flipped through a few pages, and asked, "What are the fourteen attributes of a Grapevine in communications?"

Bob started by showing off.

First, he told him the page number where the fourteen attributes were listed. Then he named all fourteen attributes in the order they appeared on that page.

The professor was dumbfounded. He relented. He gave Bob the perfect score he had earned.

As Bob created new ways to organize and retain information, he earned his first perfect 4.0 semester. His GPA jumped from a baccalaureate 3.0 to a Grad school 3.8. This was truly amazing. His educational experience transformed from one of drudgery and futility into an exciting, fulfilling adventure.

More than that, it was gratifying to make a difference in the lives of so many other students by helping them learn what he had learned about how to learn.

In the process, he discovered that he was a good teacher, a captivating presenter. He loved watching students react with amazement and delight as they realize the power and potential they had always had but were never aware of until this moment.

The great Zig Ziglar believed that one way to get experience – especially when no one will hire you – is to do it for free. That is, in fact, how Bob got started as a memory expert. Then he upped the ante by monetizing it.

Soon after graduating with his Master's degree – something he never could have done without his own customized memory system – he began thinking of all the students he had helped, for free. He asked his friend Nick Muir, an accomplished entrepreneur, if he thought students would *pay* for this?

Nick thought they would. He suggested selling it door-to-door. Bob didn't like the idea much, but Nick insisted on giving it a try. He took Bob to a copy center where they created about two hundred tickets to a memory development seminar.

Bob started selling his memory seminar to students door-to-door for twenty bucks: five dollars for the ticket for their reservation, then fifteen dollars at the door. Students could afford that, even in 1985. It worked. This was exciting!

Bob made more money in an hour working for himself than he'd ever made in a month working for someone else. *All he was doing was monetizing something he had to do for himself in order to succeed.* He started out doing it for free, then a friend helped him monetize it. He created a business that eventually brought him a six figure annual income and a lifetime career as a professional speaker.

Bob had **monetized memory**.

As much as it might seem to be, this isn't about money – not really. It is about creating financial security, financial power, peace and personal strength and confidence. It is about being able to care for yourself, your loved ones, and others who depend on you. It's about causes you want to support or promote. It is about making a difference in the world.

Most importantly, this is about enjoying life – and building the kind of financial strength that creates freedom for you and yours. Think of the comfort residual income brings. We are used to trading time for money (a job), but that's Level One thinking and that simply won't get you there.

Prosperity and peace of mind are not going to come from additional part-time jobs. There simply aren't enough hours in a day to do that. We need a different mindset. A monetized mindset so we can more effectively use the time we do have and start making money without the time-consuming effort required by hourly part time jobs.

"I always did something I was a little not ready to do. I think that's how you grow. When there's that moment of 'wow I'm not really sure I can do this' and you push through those moments, that's when you have a breakthrough."

~Marissa Mayer

Chapter Six ~
Mom-etize It

Are you a mom? Would you like to stay at home with your kids? Can't afford to do that? Gotta' work? Whether you are looking for a few hundred or a few thousand dollars a month extra (or if you would like to build a multi-million-dollar business), it is time to *Monetize Your Mindset* – or, rather, MOM-etize it!

Jamberry

Meet Keri Evans. Keri is a co-founder of Jamberry, a direct sales nail wrap company with lifetime sales of over a half a billion dollars (Jamberry.com). It started as a side hustle – a side business [BartMerrell.com/side-hustle] that within five years turned a multi-million-dollar profit – *which wasn't their goal*. This was just a project that Keri and her sisters tried out in order to have some fun and create a little extra income. That "little extra income" turned out to be millions.

Let's begin at the beginning. Nail wrapping is a process of creating a surface decal to beautify women's nails (natural or otherwise) with an intricate design, color, sparkle, etc. In 2010, the process of adding such adornment was quite expensive – forty to fifty dollars a pop – and was only provided by beauty salons.

Sometimes Keri and her sisters would visit a salon together and chit-chat while they got their nails done. One day, one of her sisters made a simple comment that changed their lives, "I bet we could make these ourselves, at home, cheaper."

They thought "Why not? Let's try it." They tried to buy product from the company that supplied their nail salon, but were turned down. The company would only sell product to a licensed nail salon. That got them curious – and probably a little stubborn.

They did some research. Was there already a company out there that did what they needed; that is, make this kind of product available to individuals? No, there wasn't. Keri's brother-in-law suggested that if they believed there would be a market for their idea or product or service, and no other company was filling or supplying the need, then they should give it a shot.

With some effort, they managed to get their hands on some nail wrap product and their research and development of DIY (do-it-yourself) nail wraps began. Four months later they had developed a prototype and some samples and were headed to their first trade show. Thus, Jamberry was born.

They didn't have actual product available for sale at the show, just some samples for people to try. They went home with a huge stack of orders. This was beyond their expectations. Actually they didn't really have any expectations; mostly hope, imagination and a willingness to work and maybe a willingness to take a modest risk to make a little extra income. They returned with so many orders, they had no idea how they were going to fill them. What a great problem to have!

They set up shop in Keri's mother's basement, outsourced the printing, then the entire family pulled together and got the orders out.

With confidence born from their initial success, they signed up for another trade show, the Christmas show. It was another outstanding success. They came home with another stack of orders. This time they were prepared to fill them – and fill them they did.

They immediately plowed the profits back into the business. One of the first things they did was buy a commercial printer. Doing their own printing instead of outsourcing it would significantly enhance their profits.

Thus far, their success had come about without much planning. However, now that they had invested a significant amount of money and personal effort into their business, they needed to stop shooting from the hip. It was time to get serious and create a business plan.

The sisters and their husbands booked a couple of hotel rooms for a few days and left for their own little business retreat. There were many issues to discuss. What would be their business model? Would they retail, wholesale, or direct market? Would they use a party style system like Pampered Chef or Tupperware? Would they establish an on-line store? They returned from their business retreat with a "party plan direct sales system" with which they built an extremely profitable company.

Their amazing success story was born in 2010 from something the sisters were already doing. Their primary motive was to just have some fun together and create a little extra income on the side. They sold the majority of the company in 2015. Their "little extra income" amounted to millions.

I asked Keri what would be her advice to people wanting to start a side hustle, I loved her answer, "Even if you don't know everything about the business, just start it, and learn as you go."

That is great advice. We'll dive into that a little deeper later in this book.

"If someone offers you an amazing opportunity and you're not sure you can do it, say yes – then learn how to do it later"
    ~ Sir Richard Branson.

Picking Up the Pieces with Greek Baklava

What happens when what happens, happens? What if what happens is a divorce? It happens. We all know it. What will you do if it happens to you and you become a single mom? Will you be able to pay your bills? Take care of your kids? Of course you will. You will be awarded child support – perhaps alimony. Everything will be just fine.

What if he doesn't pay? What will you do then?

Rita is an amazing woman. One fine Christmas Day her husband informed her that he wanted a divorce. She had a three year old son and was eight months pregnant. This was not a very merry Christmas! The next several months were miserable. Her despair lasted a relatively short time, however; she was the type to feel not helpless or hopeless for long without doing something about it. Rita had a good business sense and a history of excelling where many hadn't. This gave her hope.

She grew up in a small town in North Carolina, the fourth of five kids. She was the first of her family to attend college where she studied Spanish and Latin American culture. She went to Spain on a *Study Abroad* program to deepen her skill and understanding. There she met and married a Spaniard. They struggled financially so they decided to move to the United States, where they started a travel agency, *Amigo Travel,* which catered to the growing Latino community. It was a fairly quick success. Life was good. Rita thought she was going to live happily ever after. Not so.

After several years of what seemed like a happy marriage, establishing a great business and running it with her husband, she found herself divorced. Fortunately, she had set up the business as co-owners so, for four years after the divorce, her income continued as she ran this business together with her ex-husband. This wasn't much fun, but she didn't feel she had much of a choice because she was now a single mother of two youngsters that needed taking care of.

Four years of that kind of co-ownership and management was enough. She sold her interest in the business to her ex-husband and left. She was now on her own with two children to take care of (who were also enrolled in an expensive private school). She had tuition, mortgage payments, household expenses and other bills to pay. How was she going to meet her obligations? She needed to figure things out.

She had built businesses before and desired the freedom that owning your own business can provide, especially the opportunity of being with her children. She wanted to go down that path again.

She thought about some of the things she enjoyed doing. When she was in high school she had learned to make Greek Baklava. She was good at it. Within the regulations of the Cottage Food Program [Google "Cottage Food Program"] she was able to start *Sheer Ambrosia Bakery* and sell Greek Baklava from her home. She could work and still be with her kids – which was her main goal. Rita monetized something she liked to do.

Sheer Ambrosia Bakery grew to a point that she felt like she needed to open a retail location, which she did in the spring of 2013. After running it for three years, she realized that she had become a slave to the bakery. She was working eighteen hour days, which prevented her from being with her children as she had planned.

She put the bakery location up for sale and went back to running *Sheer Ambrosia Bakery* out of her home. Her children were elated, they loved having Mom back. Being with her children was the reason she was in business in the first place. Her intention wasn't to get rich; it was to have a home-based business that would give her the freedom to volunteer at their school when she could, and also be home when her children returned from school. *Sheer Ambrosia Bakery*, which started from something she liked to do – a culinary hobby – still brings in $25,000 to $30,000 a year.

Working out of her home gave Rita lots of time to think about life, ponder her divorce and consider how she had been able to constructively and successfully cope with it. She thought perhaps her ideas and methods, her coping strategies, might help others who were going through the same kind of experience. So, she published her thoughts in a book titled, *From Mrs. to Ms. – How To Pull Your Life Together When Your Marriage Falls Apart.*

No, she had not wanted to go through a divorce, but she managed to deal with that experience successfully and it made sense to share her thoughts with others by becoming a published author. Her experience, her ideas, her attitude and philosophy, her strategies, do help others – lots of others! Many who read the book write to her, thanking her and telling her how relieved they were to know that someone else had dealt with what they were dealing with; that someone else had the same feelings, frustrations and fears, as they had; and that someone else had survived and prospered. They thanked her for helping them know that they were not alone.

She earned a worthwhile income from sales of a book inspired by something she needed to do.

It didn't end there. Because of her book, people began ask her for specific as well as general advice. She did her best to respond in a helpful way. She saw how much her experiences were helping others; so, since she was doing it anyway, why not get out there and get paid for it? In 2016, she signed up for a course that credentialed her as a certified divorce coach.

Rita has a monetized mindset. She monetized something she liked to do (baking Greek Baklava), she monetized something that she needed to do (going through a divorce) and she is monetizing something she was already doing (coaching people through the process and aftermath of divorce).

If you would like to know more about Rita's services, here are her websites:

- Do you want some yummy Greek Baklava? Her website is SheerAmbrosiaBakery.com.
- Would you like to buy her book? Go to RitaMagalde.com.
- Do you feel you are in need of her advice? Connect with her on CompassDivorceCoaching.com.

Why does Rita live the life of an entrepreneur? Her initial reason: "To be there for my kids." She needed to do more than provide for them financially, she needed to be present, and they needed her to be present.

Did she succeed? Well, once a year, her school gives out a "Parent of the Year" award. She was the recipient several times. When I interviewed her, she told me that her intent wasn't to brag on herself, but to help others by showing how her monetized mindset empowered her to be a successful mom by creating financial circumstances that allow her to do what was most important to her – be there for her family.

Perfect Penmanship

Jenny played the piano well. She took lessons as a child, learned how to play, and also learned how to learn. She began to teach other kids, then by the time she was about sixteen years old, she started getting paid to teach. She taught for several years, continuing to teach until her two eldest children (she is the mother of four) were in their teens. Teaching piano lessons is a great side hustle for this stay-at-home mom – or at least, it was.

When her children were young, she scheduled the lessons during the time her kids took their afternoon naps. As her kids got older, however, this particular aspect of her side hustle became a bit of a problem. True, she was home with her children, which is a big part of why she had built a home-based business; to be home with her kids, but not to ignore them!

When she was teaching piano lessons, she was busy interacting with other people's children and after her kids got too old to be taking naps while she taught, she began to feel she was neglecting them a bit. They may not have felt that way, but she did; and that was what drove her to try to come up with something else.

Something interesting happened. Jenny has perfect penmanship. Her talent isn't just musical, she is artistic. It is no surprise that her perfect penmanship evolved into a decorative calligraphic style. One day she asked her now teenage son Daniel to make her a wooden box that she could decorate with her calligraphy and create a centerpiece for her table; something to put flowers in.

Several guests saw her creation and liked it. Because of their positive reactions to her art, she decided to make a few for a charity auction. They were a hit.

She wondered if she could sell them successfully, privately, so one night, she created an ad and placed it on her "neighborhood yard sale page" on Facebook. She then went to bed. When she woke up the next morning, she had orders for seventy boxes. Talk about making money while you sleep!

Jenny took it to another level. She made her first post on Instagram @madebyjen_. She told me how excited she was when her Instagram followers reached over a hundred. Now (as I write this) she has over *thirteen* hundred followers. Perhaps that doesn't seem like a lot to others, but it created a positive income stream of nearly one thousand dollars a month – and she's having fun doing it!

Jenny puts her creative calligraphy on reclaimed wood, holiday decorations, table name tags for weddings, event centerpieces, etc. (There are just too many things to list!) To see her in action and also see more of what she offers check out her Instagram @madebyjen_.

This is how *Jenny McAllister Calligraphy* began. It was a fun side hustle – a home-based business – that creates a worthwhile income stream and lets her stay connected with her children as they grow up.

The decision Jenny made to shift her side hustle from piano lessons to calligraphy created a better situation for her by enabling her to stay connected with her kids. Her business enhances her relationship with her family rather than gets in the way of it (remember, her son helped her get started by making the first centerpiece box), rather than get in the way of it. While she is working, she can chat with her kids about their day at school and whatever else is going on in their lives.

Yes, the piano lesson business was a great side hustle while her children were little, but as they got older, it created a bit of a separation, so she created a home-based business that is just as much fun as the piano lessons – maybe more fun. It provides a creative outlet for her while it allows her to interact with her children even while she is working (which, as you recall, is the main reason she wanted to create a side hustle where she could work from her home).

She develops worthy income streams doing what she would do anyway, and in this case, things she enjoyed doing (as she did with her piano lesson project); so why not get paid for it? That's a good enough reason to be doing a side hustle, right?

Well, yes, it is; and it gets better.

She has found another bonus; she gets to interact with people all over the country. When I interviewed her, she had just finished four, 2X4 wood panels for a wedding in Virginia. She said it was really fun working with this young couple, customizing their project so they got exactly what they wanted for their wedding.

She now has plans to up the ante by teaching others how to do this. She is considering conducting local, hands-on classes and perhaps doing this online as well.

Twice now, Jenny has turned something she likes to do and would do anyway into an income stream. As of this writing, she grosses over $10,000 a year doing something she enjoys and allows her to be a part of her kid's lives.

Drama Queen

Kelly says that she probably came out of the womb singing and dancing instead of kicking and screaming.

She was a consummate little actress. As a little girl, she would perform in her living room for anyone watching; or to the mirror; or to no one at all. She would sing and dance on a mini trampoline... you know, those single-person trampolines that her mother probably wanted to use as workout equipment, but never got to because little Kelly was hogging it all the time. This little trampoline was Kelly's first stage.

In the private schools she attended, drama was the cool thing to do. It was the place to be so there she was. She started acting at age ten. Then came middle school. Drama wasn't so cool anymore. Kelly didn't care. While the other kids were moving on to sports and cheerleading and glee clubs, Kelly stayed in drama.

Her love for acting grew; not just for what it did for her but for what it did for audiences. They would laugh, they would cheer, they would cry. She got to make that happen. Kelly went from school drama to community theater, continuing to grow in her craft. Then one day, it finally happened! She broke into the business – show business!

She was fourteen years old when she got her first professional paid acting gig. She was in the Disney movie "Life is Ruff." She made enough money in that two-day shoot to buy her first car. How cool is that!

She thought she had it made. This would get better and better until she was famous! Not so. It is axiomatic that actors have to wait tables to pay the bills so they can do what they love – act. Kelly didn't have to wait tables, after all, she was still in high school, but she soon realized that being a successful actress was not going to be simple or easy.

At one point she did work at a salon as a receptionist to support her acting habit. She said it was kind of painful to do something she didn't particularly enjoy, or at least wasn't passionate about, but it helped pay the bills between acting contracts.

In her twenties, she got involved with a youth theater. She found that she connected well with the younger generation. Kids and their parents started asking her if she would offer private acting classes. At first she said, "No." She wasn't even sure how to be a coach; but as she thought about it, she realized that the only way to move forward was to be willing to take a risk – to try something new even if she wasn't sure how to do it. So she changed her "no" to "yes."

She started teaching youth acting classes and found that she loved it! That began Kelly's dream side hustle (KellyECoombs.com). It was a side hustle that was directly related to doing something she loves – acting. She found she loved teaching as well. Today, she has clients all around the county that she teaches via Skype as well as local students she teaches in person.

Recently, Kelly partnered up with the Hale Center Theater, a local theater company. She teaches adult acting classes. Kelly is grateful for every second she gets to do what she loves. Perhaps even more important, she has discovered that she can do that by remaining open to possibilities and being willing to try many different mediums – acting on stage, teaching students... she even has a ball playing the princess for princess parties.

Kelly has developed a great monetized mindset. She is ever more aware of the many opportunities around her. She is willing to take action even if she is not completely sure how it will all work out. That willingness to try something even when one is unsure of how, exactly, to proceed, is key to a monetized mindset.

Passion for Fashion

Paige is an entrepreneur at heart. She enjoys the challenge of building a business, helping it grow, evolve, and thrive – then selling it to someone she feels will continue its success. She pours herself into her projects. Her side hustles aren't just random choices, they are a reflection or extension of who she is – what she cares about – what she is most interested in. That passion maintains her energy and focus and gives her staying power as she builds businesses she cares about.

She has always had, as she puts it, "a particular passion for all things fashion." Fifteen years ago, she opened a clothing store. She grew it into a profitable venture and sold it at a good profit. This was her first serious business venture. Actually it was an *ad*venture because taking the risk to create her own business, taught her much about her talents and her strengths, particularly in the ever-changing world of fashion.

Like many others before her, Paige discovered that, more often than not, a person's interests are linked to their talents. What are Paige's strengths? What are her talents? Early in life, she identified two strengths or traits that that make this happen: #1 she seems to inspire peoples' confidence in themselves as well as in her; #2 she has a natural ability to break down barriers between people and groups and turn awkward situations into comfortable, productive situations. Those seemed to be her strengths, and when she combined them with what she cared about, her interests and passions, she seemed to tap into a wellspring of energy and focus that carried her through the difficult times that always seem to accompany the development of any business.

Paige leads her business activities with her strengths – particularly her passion for fashion. They in turn led *her* in a direction she did not initially suspect.

In 2011, Paige built an essential oils business, using a direct sales business model. This was not easy for her. While she loves the product (she uses the oils every day) she lacks passion for the direct sales industry.

In 2014 Paige decided to fuse her passions together and she created "Fashion and Oils." It seemed the perfect combination – for her. She adopted the title Fashion Stylist & Image Consultant in a unique way; she develops healthy living and a sense of style from the inside out.

This unique combination of interests breathed life into the essential oils aspect of her business. It allowed her to do what she loved while still funneling interested people into her essential oils business. Her business began to flourish.

Paige loves what she gets to do every day. She enhanced her consulting business by focusing on clients who are in the public eye; in front of large audiences, on stage, and on television. It has opened many exciting doors for her. Paige has had the opportunities to dress and re-brand female business professionals who are often in the spotlight. She helps them think outside the typical "business professional look." Many of her clients have awesome personalities and are so much more than a boring pant suit. They are creative, fun, funny and bold and have much to offer the world. She helps them look the part.

Paige's clients are able to enhance their personal and presentation style through a more effective use of fashion. This helps them develop and strengthen their image and thereby strengthen their connection with their audiences and other clientele.

Paige's success demonstrates that an important, if not essential, part of *Monetizing Your Mindset* is to pay attention to what you are best at, and most passionate about. Whether your passion is for fashion, art, mechanics or gardening, focus on the things you like and are good at and build your business(es), your side hustles, around what you enjoy the most. As much as anything else, this will enhance and maintain your energy, your focus, and your success. If you would like to connect with Paige, here is how to do so.

Paige Sorensen
@stylelifewithpaige
stylelifewithpaige@gmail.com

Making Homes out of Houses

Age is not a detriment to your ability to monetize your mindset. It is never too late to become financially secure. The key is to understand what is required and do it. Age can provide the wisdom and experience needed to do it right.

Enter Carolyn, the homemaker who makes homes from houses.

Carolyn started developing her monetized mindset later in life. She already had the foundations and framework for a monetized mind because she had experimented in several home-based businesses over the years, so developing the mindset came pretty naturally.

Her side hustles ranged from paper routes to cooking classes and shows; home party and other direct sales projects. They were not a waste of time, exactly, because she learned much but, at the end of the day, she realized her efforts weren't particularly profitable. She had been trading time for money and her trades hadn't been particularly good ones. There wasn't enough return on investment (ROI) for the time spent.

Her paper route, for example, which she started for her kids to learn some business sense and personal responsibility, turned into what amounted to a full time job for *her* – a full time job with part time pay – and no benefits.

Her day started around four in the morning, with the paper route, and pushed all her other responsibilities back so her day didn't end until eleven or twelve at night.

"I was constantly tired" She said. "There were times I was so exhausted I could close my eyes and fall asleep in two seconds – literally. And I didn't have to close my eyes voluntarily; they would just shut on their own.
When I came to a stop light, I worried that I would fall asleep and roll into the intersection or hit the car ahead of me.

All this just to make a little extra money? And that's exactly what I did. I made 'a little extra money.' The operational word? 'Little.' It barely covered the mileage it took to deliver the papers. It was inefficient. It was brutal."

Carolyn also worked a part-time job as a seamstress, which turned into sixty-plus hours a week. This wasn't exactly a side hustle, but it had the same lack of benefits or decent pay. It provided an income stream that, after expenses, taxes, etc., was a mere trickle. If it had been a passive income stream, that would be fine, but she had to work daily to get paid weekly – paid a pittance compared to the hours she invested.

She knew her time was more valuable than that. She needed a much better ROI (return on her investment) on her time if she was ever going to get ahead.

Carolyn was certainly not lazy. She was a hard worker, a conscientious provider but relatively ineffectual in terms of ROI. That was not the example she wished to create for her children.

Carolyn also realized that working herself into the ground for little income was creating a constant state of "want" in her family. She did not want her children to be conditioned with a feeling of lack.

She knew that in order to set a better example for her kids she needed to find better side hustles that created passive income streams – or at least income streams that would not drown her in work that produced a poor return. Her time/money equation wasn't working. That had to change.

She wanted her children to learn not only a sense of responsibility but also a sense of prosperity; to understand that there were opportunities all around them that could create financial security. That is the mindset she wanted her children to grow up with. She began a search for a side hustle that would help her be the example she wanted to be for her kids.

She set out to find something that was not affected so much by the economy – or maybe actually could benefit from a poor economy (like Thomas Cantrell's side hustle that became a career that actually thrives during periods of high unemployment and economic distress). She wanted something that would always be relevant, profitable, worthy of her investment of time, regardless of economic circumstances.

That led her to think about real estate. Rich or poor, good economy or bad, people always need a place to live. Additionally, business people tend to value real estate investments. Even after the crash of 2008, land is still considered a well-grounded investment (pun clearly intended).

A little research revealed that when the economy is good, business people look for property in which to invest their money. If the economy is bad, these same people are looking to snatch up good real estate deals.

However, the real estate market felt intimidating to her. It seemed too complex for her. She just didn't believe, or at least she didn't know if, she could do it. Even if she could do it, she wasn't sure where or how to start.

Doubt was a detriment. Following close on the heels of doubt, though was determination. "If others can do this, why couldn't I?" She simply had to roll up her sleeves and get to work. So, in her mid-fifties, Carolyn decided to "just dive in and learn to swim."

Job one was figuring out *what* to do. People with a monetized mindset surround themselves with and learn from people who are already doing what it is that they want to do. Carolyn began the process by seeking out and associating with people who were involved, in any way, with real estate.

"It was quite daunting," Carolyn said, "going from a stay-at-home mom to jumping into the high-powered business world dominated by men. But I did it. I decided and learned by doing."

Iconic management consultant and well known author, professor Peter F. Drucker said, "Whenever you see a successful business, someone once made a courageous decision." That is exactly what Carolyn did. She made a courageous decision to swim with the sharks and dove right in.

She figured out how to converse with people about money, partnering and establishing trust where large sums of money are involved. She learned to talk to people who were selling their own property, find out what they had to deal with, what their unique problems, concerns, even their fears, were; and how to discover, figure out and provide solutions for the sellers.

She also learned about the process of 'rehabbing' a house and how to estimate the construction and other costs associated with transforming a house into a home. She learned how far she could trust contractors and subcontractors and what to do when they don't live up to their part of the agreement.

Carolyn bought her first income property in her late fifties. It was a house from a grandmother who was moving into a retirement community. The older woman was no longer able to take care of the house nor was she in a position to renovate it to get it ready to sell. In addition, her grandkids were living with her and she did not have the heart to kick them out. She felt stuck.

Then Carolyn came along. Carolyn's experience as a homemaker – and a mom – were unexpected assets. They helped her create a connection with the homeowner. The grandmother trusted her and she and Carolyn agreed on a fair price. Carolyn bought the house and took on the job of being the bad guy and telling the grandchildren they had to leave.

The renovation began. It was an inside/out job. Fresh paint, new light fixtures and appliances, updated bathroom... then outside paint, roof renovation, landscaping... This house received a facelift and a tummy tuck! Soon it was like new again, inside and out. This was gratifying, rewarding, profitable! This was indeed a worthy investment of Carolyn's time and money.

We have talked about creating side hustles by monetizing...

1 ~ What we like to do,

2 ~ What we need to do,

3 ~ What we are already doing...

At first, real estate didn't seem to fit in any of these three categories, but in actuality, it did. Directly or indirectly it involved something Carolyn liked to do, needed to do and was doing anyway – being a home-maker.

Carolyn "mom-etized" real estate.

Her ability to communicate with all kinds of potential buyers (older people trying to downsize, younger growing families looking for a homes to buy or rent) became a huge asset. Because she was a homemaker herself, she had an eye for what someone would like to live in, not just invest in. She didn't just upgrade and remodel, she would make a house a home.

She made that grandmother happy, helped beautify the neighborhood, created incomes for contractors and others, enhanced neighborhoods and created a more liveable home for a family. She created income streams for herself and her family. She taught her children better habits of thinking, enhancing their perception and understanding of how to create a secure income. This side hustle, this new career, was not just a win-win, it was a win-win-win-win-win.

Carolyn's says it this way, "Moms – women – tend to be social creatures. We thrive on being with other people. A good side hustle can provide opportunity to socialize outside of the home while still maintaining connection to family. Having multiple streams of income in today's world where things can change in an instant, is a necessity. A side hustle like mine provides that outlet, helps me maintain my connection with my family, and allows me to get paid at the same time.

In the end, what Carolyn loves about her career in real estate investing and renovation is that it utilizes her natural and her developed talents for being a mother, a wife, a homemaker, as she creates homes from houses.

"Find a job you enjoy doing and you'll never work a day in your life."

~ Mark Twain

Chapter Seven ~
Follow your Passion (or not)

Billionaire Mark Cuban said in an interview, "One of the great lies of life is 'follow your passions.'"

What an uneducated statement.

Wait! Who I am I to call Mark Cuban uneducated? He is a billionaire. He must be smarter than me. Yes, he very well may be smarter than me, but his statement is not well thought out. He did, in fact, follow his passion – at least one of them. He seems to be unaware that he did that.

Why shouldn't we follow our passions? Mark Cuban and I share a passion: basketball. I played basketball in high school but not very well. I reached 6'4" as a senior. I was always big for my age so I played both in junior high and high school. But I didn't do very well. I simply didn't have the right physical configuration.

I have a long torso and short legs. I represent the perfect stereotypical player with the debilitating "white man's disease:" *White Men Can't Jump.* It's true – for me, at least. I cannot jump to save my life, and I can't run very fast either.

I really do love basketball. I am just no good at it. I tried out every year in high school, and every year, the first week or two of basketball practice was pure hell. I threw up every day. It would be laughable for me to think I would ever make it into the NBA. The chances would be a million to one.

Lloyd from the movie, *Dumb and Dumber* would say, "So you're telling me there's a chance." Well in my case, not so much. Mark may have had a similar experience.

Here's the question: Do I have to become an NBA player to make money with my passion for basketball? No. Neither does Mark Cuban. There are many other ways he and I can profit from our passion. I could monetize it if I wanted to. Mark already has.

True, Mark did not get rich playing basketball. Maybe that's why he says what he says about following your passion being a lie. He says "I used to be passionate about being a professional basketball player – but then I realized I had only a seven inch vertical [jump]."

What if he had reinterpreted his passion or slanted it a bit into the cognition that he was passionate about the game whether or not he was any good at *playing* the game?

My beekeeper and speaker friend Brad Barton is also a world-record-breaking runner. He is passionate about track and field. His coach, Chick Hislop, is also passionate about track and field.

Brad achieved international fame as a runner. Chick Hislop achieved international fame as a coach, even though he was never a champion athlete. He will, in fact, tell you he is a lousy athlete. Chick's passion for track and field helped him *create* champions, including at least one world champion athlete – so far. He was inducted into the Hall of Fame because of his success in getting the best out of the best.

Coach Hislop monetized his passion for track and field (including writing a successful book about it[2]) even though he never won a race in his life.

So, isn't it the same for Mark Cuban? He likely never made a dime *playing* basketball, but he does make a lot of money in business activities directly involving his passion: basketball. Mark monetized his passion for basketball by buying a professional basketball team – the Dallas Mavericks.

What about me? I'm just as passionate about basketball as Mark is. While it is not likely that I will ever buy a professional team like he did, there are other options – many other ways I could monetize my passion for basketball – many that perhaps haven't even been discovered yet.

[2]   *On Track* by Coach Chick Hislop ~ Publisher: iPrimedia ~ E-launch LLC, 2016 ISBN 1684183790, 9781684183791
https://books.google.com/books/about/On_Track.html?id=sVd6vgAACAAJ

That is what Mark Cuban did. He just doesn't realize it. He did, in fact, follow his passion by monetizing his love for basketball.

In another interview Mark Cuban says, "If you find something that you like to do – love to do – be great at it and try to turn it into a business. Worst case you are going to have fun doing something you like to do; best case you turn it into a business [a stream of income]."

He thought out this statement a little better, didn't he? So should we? Follow our passions? Worst case scenario? You are going to have fun doing something you like to do. Best case scenario? You will turn your passion into a business which will create a stream of income for you, just as so many others have done.

Mark Cuban was right about becoming a professional athlete. It is tough. You have to be the best of the best to make it. Natural talent and great body structure help a lot. But to be successful as an entrepreneur, you don't need to be the best of the best; it isn't really competitive as most make it out to be. You need effort, consistency, activity, and consistent awareness – and you will win.

So, how about you?

What do you *like* to do?
What do you *need* to do?
What are you *already* doing?

Let's monetize it.

"People rarely succeed unless they have fun in what they are doing."

~ Dale Carnegie

Chapter Eight ~
Monetize What You Like to Do

What do you like to do?
What do you need to do?
What are you already doing?

I like music...

No, I *love* music. I always have.

I bought my first stereo at age eleven. I worked all summer on the farm to save up the $285 needed to buy a Sanyo all-in-one system. It was awesome! It had the cassette deck on the left side, the 8-track on the right (yes, I did say 8-track. If you don't know what that is, then Google it), the AM/FM radio in the middle, and a turntable on top to play vinyl records (Google might be necessary here too).

Little did I know that this penchant for music would cost me a lot more than $285. I became addicted to music. I had to have all the new tunes. Every time we went to town, I bought more music. It soon became a liability. All my money was going to music. It was an expensive hobby (remember, hobbies *cost* you money, businesses *make* you money).

Something had to change. No, I did not stop buying music. I did not give up my passion. I embraced it – leaned in to it. I turned it into a business. Brad monetized honey. Thomas monetized conflict. Bob monetized memory.

I monetized music!

At age fifteen, because of the monetized mindset my father had instilled in me, I figured out how to monetize music. Others have done that, but they are singers and musicians. I can't hold a note in a bucket and I'm not a composer, but I do love music, so I decided to start a mobile disco business.

There was just one small problem. Nobody was hiring. There were not many events in our small town that required disc jockeys.

Perhaps there were no events, but *could* there be? *Should* there be? I thought so. As it turned out, so did the public. I took a risk. I tried something. I rented the community center and announced a community dance. I hired an off-duty cop for security, Mom and Dad took money at the door, and I spun records. Everyone danced and had great fun.

I netted three to five hundred dollars a night from monetizing music! I monetized something that I loved. It was fun – and it paid off. What a concept! I got paid for having fun, and I got paid pretty well, too!

I continued to invest and reinvest in my business. Within a few months, I had a killer sound system. It was rockin'! Dual amps; Peavey speakers; light system… It was great fun!

At age fifteen, I had monetized fun.

I was passionate about music. I had been spending money on music. I was playing music anyway. I simply monetized something I liked to do and was doing already anyway. I didn't just seize an opportunity that came along. I created my opportunity by putting on my own event – a community dance.

This was the first time I ever did anything like this on my own. Sure, I had monetized certain natural skills, like getting paid to shovel pig poop on my dad's pig farm. I was not passionate about shoveling manure, but I earned enough doing that to buy something I *was* passionate about – music.

If my father hadn't helped me develop a mind for monetization, it would have ended with my music business, but that process of monetizing something I loved (music) and was investing in anyway (the sound system) had an ongoing ripple effect that changed my life by changing the way I view everything I do.

Specifically, when I do something, like buy a house or a truck or whatever, my brain, operated by my monetized mind, automatically kicks out the question, could I monetize that? More specifically, *how* can I monetize that?

The profits from the music business gave me spending money in high school and financed most of my first two years of college.

The investment grew.

By the time I neared the end of my second year of college, the business was worth twenty thousand dollars. I sold my interests. And moved on…

This is the Level Two I spoke of earlier in this book. I was monetizing a set of skills I developed from an interest in something I loved to do. I wasn't working for a wage; I was selling my services directly to the public.

Monetized Passion for Big Trucks

Years later, I was in Japan working on a business project. I was new to the area and had not made any friends yet other than from work. I focused on the business during the day. At night I was left without much to do. To kill time and get in shape, I began to run a few miles a day. That got boring, so I found a gym close to where I lived. I had nothing much else to do, so I would hit the gym almost every night.

I had been going there for just over a week when I met Atsumi. Because I was different – the big American guy – I was probably a little overwhelming for the other gym members to approach. No one really talked to me, beyond a polite greeting or a nod. Then, out of the blue this guy came up to me and said, "Harro!" (hello)

I replied, "Wha'su'p," then, "konichiwa," which is Japanese for "harro."

He had barely completed high school, and had done so with less than stellar grades. He did not speak a lick of English – except for "harro." He told me later he was glad I spoke Japanese because if I hadn't, the conversation wouldn't have gone any further than "harro."

We continued our conversation in Japanese. Atsumi was not your typical Japanese person. He was as tall as I am, 6'4" and slender. He wore cowboy boots and Wrangler jeans. He loved trucks. He was a professional big-rig driver in Japan. His personal vehicle was a white, lifted, four-wheel-drive Dodge Ram pickup. He was a down-home country boy with Japanese roots. He loved American country-western music, Harley Davidson motorcycles, and, of course, his Dodge truck.

A couple of years after we first met, Atsumi told me that he wanted to quit driving the big rig that he owned and drove professionally and start importing camp trailers and Ford and Dodge pickups (something he was passionate about) from America to Japan. He asked if I would partner up and help him. We started that partnership in 1997 and have been working together ever since.

Atsumi did not have a strong formal education but he was smart and had the guts to monetize what he was passionate about. Today he imports trucks, trailers, Harleys, and parts for the like.

He monetized something he was passionate about (his truck) and loved doing (driving his truck), then added something else he loved (Harley-Davidson Motorcycles and related parts). That is the beginning of Atsumi's monetized mindset.

In her hit song, Tina Turner asks an important question "What's Love Got to Do with It?" What does love have to do with making money?

Reportedly, Confucius suggested that if you do what you love, you never have to work a day in your life. Whether Confucius actually said something like that, there is much truth to the statement. You may be working very hard, but if you love it, it doesn't feel like work.

It goes beyond that. When you monetize something you enjoy, love, are passionate about: like making music, driving trucks and motorcycles, keeping bees, arguing legal concepts, learning to learn, riding horses, etc., you may find yourself creating more than just an extra stream of income and even more than a business. You may well find yourself stepping into the world of unlimited income and making a difference in this world – and loving life!

"Success is a little like wrestling a gorilla. You don't quit when you're tired. You quit when the gorilla is tired."

~ Robert Strauss

Chapter Nine ~
Monetize What You Need to Do

What do you like to do?
What do you need to do?
What are you already doing?

You need to have somewhere to live, right? You can rent or you can buy. After college, a friend and I instead of paying rent ourselves we rented a house, took the rooms we wanted and sublet the other rooms to cover the rent. Sounds pretty intelligent, right? No, it wasn't. We were still throwing money away. Renting together and subletting rooms was good idea and pretty cost-effective, but we were still renting – making house payments for someone else and gaining zero equity.

That gave my monetized mind a migraine.

So my friend and I bought a house and rented out the extra rooms. We were doing the same thing as before, but this time we were paying rent to ourselves. Actually we weren't paying at all, we were living free. Others were paying us. The rent from the other rooms paid the mortgage, and we lived rent free.

No more throwing money down a rabbit hole.

People think that their home is an asset. It is not. Until it is paid off, it is a liability. Every month there is that little thing called a *mortgage* that comes due. Even after it is paid off you still have to pay property taxes every year.

When I got married and we were looking to buy our first home together, we specifically looked for a home that had an accessory apartment so that our home could provide a source of income.

The need to buy a house triggered my monetized mind with thoughts of how I could make money doing this. The obvious answer was to buy with the idea of selling later. The less obvious answer was to buy a home with a rental unit that would make us an additional income that would pay, or help pay, the mortgage payments. This isn't something most people think of, but my wife and I are not most people. We have a monetized mindset.

Currently our accessory apartment pays almost half of our mortgage.

I have monetized music, weight loss, bungee jumping, speaking Japanese, real estate home purchase....

I even monetized my truck.

Monetizing a Monster Machine

Business has its ups and downs. I hit a hard down. I lost $205,000 on a deal gone bad. I was headed straight into bankruptcy.

So I decided to buy a new truck.

What? I'm going broke, so I want to buy a new truck? Well, yes. I had to have transportation anyway, right? So why not by a top-of-the-line truck that could save me from bankruptcy.

Sound crazy? It's not – not to someone with a monetized mindset.

It started in late 2001. I was awakened by a call from my best friend at around eight o'clock in the morning. He said, "Bart, I'm at the FBI office, and you need to get down here right away."

Talk about a "wake up call!" That kind of call shocks you wide awake pretty fast. If it had been April Fool's Day it would have been funny, but it wasn't April Fool's Day, and it wasn't funny.

I didn't even take time for a shower. I got dressed, hopped into my late model Toyota and headed down to the office of the Federal Bureau of Investigation, just a few blocks away. I had no idea the FBI office was so close to my house, but it was.

About a year earlier, I had invested a good chunk of money, $205,000, to be exact – with a fellow I had met through a friend. At the FBI office, I was informed that more than likely I had lost my entire investment.

I felt like I had just been punched in the gut so hard I was going to throw up. Nearly a quarter of a million dollars is a lot of money. What was I going to do? Buy a forty thousand dollar truck? What was wrong with me? Nothing. I have a monetized mindset.

I am a cowboy at heart. I love trucks. At the time I owned a Toyota Camry because of the gas mileage. But I really do look better in a truck! I was already in the camping trailer business, exporting them to Japan with Atsumi. I knew that there was also money to be made pulling trailers from manufacturers to dealers all over the United States.

I was making payments on a vehicle anyway. I had to drive something anyway. I needed to make more money. My monetized mindset decided to turn my personal transportation into an income stream of instead of a liability.

Please understand that because of the $205,000 loss, I was baby steps away from bankruptcy. Most smart people would pull back, be a little conservative… well, I was careful, yes, but conservative? No. My monetized mindset took the wheel, so to speak. Instead of giving into the disaster, I faced the dilemma; in fact, I stepped into it. There wasn't much room on the ledge I was standing on but there was some, so – of course – curiosity made me step closer to the edge. How could I monetize this madness?

I went to a truck dealership, and, with my good credit (not yet affected by my current financial debacle), I snagged a brand new $41,000 Ford F-350 Crew Cab.

I didn't even have a contract to pull trailers yet. It was a classic "Catch 22". I really couldn't justify buying the truck unless I had the contract to pull trailers, but sure as God made little green apples I wasn't going to get the contract unless I had the truck. So I got the truck. (Remember, I look really good in a big truck, so, what th' heck!)

Man, I wasn't just stepping close to the edge; I was now hanging off the edge by my fingertips. In my monetized mind, however, it made perfect sense to buy the truck.

My wife hoped my mind knew what it was doing!

I pulled trailers nationwide for four years. I put 290,000 miles on that truck in two and a half years. Then I sold it to a guy in Japan for $5,000 more than what I owed on it.

That gave me enough for a down payment, so I went back to the Ford store and bought another new truck. In a year and half, I put over 100,000 miles on that truck and I sold that truck in Japan for a profit as well.

Ah, yes… the amazing, mental machinations of a madman with a monetized mindset!

If I had not stepped out to the edge and hung over it to buy that first truck, that $205,000 loss would have put me into bankruptcy. Instead I came out ahead. Yes, of course it took a lot of hard work and a bunch of miles driving cross-country, but I came out ahead with a great credit rating, thanks to my dad planting the seeds of monetization in my mind.

Others have monetized something they didn't necessarily love to do but because… well, they simply needed to do it.

Signs of the Times

My friend Joe has monetized signs. When he created his company, Black Canyon Signs, Joe had not been looking to create a sign company, he just needed signs.

He owned a construction company. He needed directional signs, caution signs, advertising signs – the works. He realized that he could make his own, and save money.

Joe bought a big printer and started making his own signs. It didn't stop there. He started selling his services to other construction companies. soon, he began to add profit to his savings. His monetized mindset gave birth to Black Canyon Signs.

He monetized in two ways. First, he saved money by creating his own signs, then he created the sign company and began to make money. Benjamin Franklin would say it is all the same. Ben is probably right.

Joe was not necessarily passionate about signs but he needed signs, and started doing it for himself; so why not do it for others? Joe is always interested in finding new ways of making money and creating other income streams. This is the essential trait of someone with a monetized mindset.

"There has never been a better time, in the history of time, than right now to start a business."

~ Gary Vaynerchuk

Chapter Ten ~
What are You Already Doing?

What do you like to do?
What do you need to do?
What are you already doing?

How about Monetizing your Mutt?

I love dogs. I have had dogs all my life. If I could monetize a mongrel or mastiff or any 'ol mangy mutt, that would be monetizing something I love. Not to mention, monetizing something I am already doing – which is enjoying my dogs – and spending a whole lot of money on them!

Surely there must be some way to monetize those mongrels (my dog Diesel just raised his head and is staring at me. I wonder if he could tell that I just called him a mongrel). Actually, Diesel is a beautiful Rottweiler and his "sister" Pebbles is a wonderful Dalmatian/Blue Heeler. I really enjoy those two, as I have always enjoyed my dogs.

When I moved from the farm to the city, I took my love of dogs, and my dog, with me. Somewhere along the way, I had fallen in love with the Rottweiler breed. I bought my first Rotti pup when I was still in college. His name was Yakuza. Yakuza is the name of the Japanese mafia. It wasn't because he was vicious or violent, though he did look a bit intimidating; he was not dangerous at all. He was a gentle, fun loving companion – my hiking and fishing buddy.

In Japan, the Yakuza weren't as scary to me as the term "Japanese mafia" implies, at least not in the area in which I lived. Similarly, my dog, Yakuza, looked and sounded a lot scarier than he was. Many feel that Rottweilers are fundamentally dangerous, killers born to fight and guard. Hollywood hasn't done much to soften that image!

Yakuza was a great dog and an awesome buddy. He'd go fishing, hiking, and driving through the mountains with me. He sometimes even accompanied me on an outdoor date – like a picnic – just to get him out and about. My dates liked him. Sometimes they liked him better than they liked me!

Rottweilers are beautiful animals; muscular, naturally powerful shoulders and chest, with a huge head. They are known for their herding and guarding and are bred to enhance such traits.

They are also often viewed as dangerous. There are many references to that effect which are, in my opinion, as irresponsible as they are inaccurate. Any breed can exhibit dangerous behavior. Chihuahuas are notorious for being aggressive, protective, and snappish (and, yes, those cuddly cute little mutts can draw blood), but they are also considered emotional comfort dogs. Frankly, I'd feel a lot more comfort from a friendly, cuddly Rottweiler that could also take an intruder's head off!

Rottweilers are loyal and protective, but are typically not temperamental or aggressive. Unless they have been specifically bred and/or trained otherwise, they are actually pussycats. Rottweilers are beautiful (to me), big friendly, intelligent, playful, and happy to do anything we are doing.

Yes, they can be aggressive and dangerous. But it's the same with any canine, and is usually a result of irresponsible care, neglect, abuse – or simply a lack of proper socialization, kind of like me. I'm a pretty big fellow, but I'm not dangerous – I've been trained.

I bought Yakuza when I was back home after most of my college was completed. When I decided to go back to school, I took him with me, of course. 'Kuza was my buddy.

My apartment at college didn't allow dogs but there was a vacant lot right next to my apartment with trees and bushes. I brought some fencing up from the farm, and I made 'Kuza a dog run right next to my apartment complete with a big dog house. I don't know who owned the property, but 'Kuza lived there, rent-free, for several months while I finished my last quarter of school.

He was my "man's best friend" for over thirteen years. He died on Christmas Day, 2005. It was a sad day.

After that, most of the dogs I adopted were Rottweilers – Tank, Kati, Diesel – all great dogs. My wife and I love them (she also shares my passion about dog rescue).

Like kids, dogs represent an expense as well as a pleasure because of food, medical care, etc. I have often thought about monetizing my love of dogs, but I have never made it happen – not yet.

But someone else did. They monetized their relationship with their cute, goofy little dachshund.

Enter Crusoe the Celebrity Dachshund.

About two years ago, cute little videos of a photogenic Dachshund (if that is even possible) named Crusoe started to show up on social media. He was dressed up in different costumes doing funny little acts and antics. He has been featured as a sea captain, a vacationer on a beach drinking coconut milk, Santa Claus in a sleigh bringing doggie toys to dogs at the humane society (I wonder if they leave this Canine Claus doggie treats and milk), a downhill skier, hockey player, airplane pilot, fireman, and a patrolman (with a donut and coffee fastened to the hood of his police car).

In one video, he was dressed in construction gear complete with orange and yellow vest with reflective fabric and a yellow hard hat. He had a companion named Oakley, and they were digging a hole under the direction of a lazy human foreman. In another video, they are dressed in hunting gear, complete with shotguns and binoculars; they are hunting turkey.

Crusoe and his partner Oakley have been featured as cooks, beekeepers, winter rabbit hunters, Star Wars Storm Troopers, pedestrians, braving the rain with raincoat and umbrella, tennis players, golfers (they hit that ball then, like dogs, chase the ball after they've hit it), and, of course, patrons of "the Dog House" a bar for dogs that looks like a bathroom (the patrons drink from little toilets, of course).

These dogs, or at least the love of them, have been monetized, as has the fun of dressing them up.

How?

It started with their owners, Ryan and Laurence, doing something they were doing anyway. They had to dress Crusoe in coats and sweaters to keep him warm in the frigid winters in Ottawa Canada. Crusoe loved the clothes.

My dog, Pebbles, shares their love of clothes. She loves the doggie sweater we put on her when we walk her in the winter. When she gets home, she dodges our efforts to take the sweater off, so we leave it on her almost all the time in the winter (maybe she's just modest). I haven't monetized this – yet.

Ryan and Laurence started getting creative with the clothing and began taking pictures of Crusoe in the outfits and posting them on Facebook. People responded. Crusoe enjoyed being dressed up – he was so cute and funny in the pictures; they were "liked" and eventually went viral. While my dog Pebbles likes to be dressed for warmth, she's not yet a supermodel like Crusoe and Oakley; but maybe there's still a chance.

The still pictures of those two mutts evolved into videos. The dogs seem to enjoy the activity and the attention, and, dozens of videos later, their owners have created their own fan club – "Cru's Crew." At the time of this writing, their Facebook fan page has over 2.3 million likes.

Yes, okay, it's popular; but how do they *monetize* this?

They sell products online. You can buy a Crusoe calendar (choose from three different ones – or buy them all, of course). They offer Crusoe coffee mugs, a Crusoe coffee table book with stories, photos and recipes by Chef Crusoe. You can buy Crusoe leggings (four different choices), autographed (pawgraphed) photos, T-shirts, and pet costumes.

This is a great example of monetizing something you are already doing.

It started by accident. The dogs' owners dressed them to keep them warm in the winter (something they needed to do and were doing anyway) like my wife and I do with Pebbles.

They started taking pictures and posting them. Taking pictures of them and posting them was something the owners were doing anyway, just for fun.

They just monetized something they were already doing and enjoyed. In addition, dressing the dogs was something they needed to do, for their pets' health and safety.

By the time you read this, I am certain I will also have figured out a way to monetize my relationship with my dogs.

In the meantime, I monetized fear.

Monetizing Fear

When you sit in an exit row on an airplane do you ever think you are actually going to have to act in an emergency? Of course not. We hardly pay attention to the flight attendants when the emergency instructions are read. We just like the extra leg room. Besides, there likely won't ever *be* an emergency, right?

When the flight attendant gives you emergency instructions, do you tune them out? Does anybody really ever pay attention to emergency instructions, unless of course it's Southwest Airlines, which has an exceptionally entertaining and funny flight attendant reading the safety instructions?

I'm six-foot-four in my stocking feet. I head for the exit row seats of course. It is a little frightening that the people in the exit rows are there because they are big and tall, not because they are smart.

If there is a possible emergency, maybe a little rough air, and the pilot announces the fasten seat belt announcement while we're still at thirty thousand feet, we start thinking, "Oh crap! I should have paid more attention. What is it I am supposed to do?!" We fumble quickly for the pamphlet, usually it's just a fold over card, flip it open and speed-read it, trying to figure out what we have to do in case the situation at hand turns into a real emergency.

I was on such a flight several years ago. It was a short Salt Lake to Reno flight. Because of my height, not my relative brilliance, I vied for and won an exit row seat. Landing in Reno can be a bit of a joy ride. The wind shears sometimes require even the most experienced pilot to take two or three approaches to land safely.

Wind shear is also referred to as "wind gradient," they are winds that blow from the top – or from the side. Wind shears change speed and direction dramatically. They can create a rocky ride. For me, and for people like me, it is a "fun" ride!

As we approached the runway – in fact were only thirty feet off the ground – the plane, likely a Boeing 737, suddenly began to rock dramatically from side to side, fishtailing left and right, bouncing up and down. It was out of control, a rank, bucking bull.

The pilot accelerated, nosed the plane up, circled the airport and came in for a second approach.

Once again the plane started to rock back and forth, bucking and bouncing…

The pilot accelerated again, nosed back into the air, circled the airport and made a third pass.

Third time's a charm, right?

Nope.

Six times the pilot tried. Six times he failed.

Passengers were terrified; and, yes, there was indeed a tall person in the exit row speed-reading the emergency landing instructions. That tall person speed-reading his way through the pamphlet wasn't me, by the way. I was too busy having a blast! I am an adrenaline junkie. I leaned over to the person next to me and said, "Isn't this great! Some people pay good money for a ride like this!"

I don't recall the white-faced response, exactly.

Here was a bonus a thrill ride, truly worth the price of the ticket.

By the sixth pass, the plane began to get a little low on fuel, so we were rerouted to Sacramento to refuel. We flew an hour and change one way just to refuel so we could fly back to Reno to try and land again.

At the Sacramento International Airport, the landing was a lot less exciting. I suppose the pilot wanted us to know he really could land a plane. He wanted to prove that the *wind* was creating the problem, not him. The landing was smooth as silk – Japanese silk, of course.

Nevertheless, eleven passengers decided that Sacramento was close enough to Reno to drive back. They would rather rent a car and drive back than risk that ride again. So they exited the plane.

The problem was that the drive back to Reno would take them over Donner Pass in the Sierra Nevada Mountains. It is important to understand that this was February, the dead of winter. Donner Pass is well known as a dangerous place. A wagon train lead by George Donner in the mid-1800s became immobilized there because of the severity of the weather. They were snowed in for five months. Several of that party turned to cannibalism in order to survive.

Those eleven passengers would still rather drive through this pass even with a "severe winter warning," than risk the fun of a second Reno landing.

The rest of us rode the plane back to Reno. We landed safely in one pass. It was a smooth landing; not nearly as much fun as the earlier six attempts.

Fun? *Fun?* Risking death by plane is fun? Yes. It's as much fun as a bungee jump – from the top of an eight story tower, only holding on to the cord with your bare hands.

Who would be dumb enough to do that?

Me.

As I told you, I monetized fear.

Have you ever *been* bungee jumping?

That's where one experiences, *and pays for* (hence the monetizing), a sense of impending doom, a brush with death, a defiance of the laws of gravity, a denial of the instinct to survive. Just as I said, *fun!*

Do you know where this brilliant idea of bungee jumping came from?

An ancient ritual called "Ngol" originated on Pentecost Island in the Coral Sea in the South Pacific. Pentecost Island is north of New Zealand, somewhat east and slightly north of Australia, and southwest of New Guinea. It is, essentially, in the middle of nowhere.

Ngol is referred to as "land diving" there because participants dive headfirst off the top of high, rickety, flexible tower straight at the ground with non-OSHA (Occupational Safety and Health Administration) approved jungle vines attached to their ankles.

Yes, 'jungle vines'.

The object is to strike your shoulders on the ground just hard enough to feel it, but not enough to break your back or neck. At least that is the plan – and it works – usually.

Land diving is considered proof of bravery and the gateway to manhood. Depending on the height of the jump and the age of the diver, it proves one worthy to become *bwahri* (warrior) and enter the gates of manhood (provided you survive the jump).

Twenty to thirty-meter-high wooden towers are constructed by the villagers. Initiates climb the towers where tree vines are tied around each ankle. The length and strength of the vines are customized to each diver, based on height and weight. This is done, not by any scientific measurements but according to the wisdom and experience of village elders. This "land diving" is done without any safety equipment – unless tree vines could properly be called "safety equipment."

The diver crosses his arms over his chest to help prevent injury to the arms. He bows his head, tucking his chin into his chest so his shoulders can brush the ground. Taking this jump will prove he is a real man. (Aren't you glad you don't have to prove your courage and maturity this way?) The risk of broken neck, concussion and/or death is real. Therefore, before diving, the participants often take care of unfinished business and settle any disputes.

At some point along the way, someone watching this insane activity got an equally insane idea. This looks like fun. Not necessarily for him, of course, but for someone else with money who would enjoy jumping headfirst toward the ground with nothing but vines or some such thing tied to their ankles to break their fall, just before they broke their neck.

Who would pay to do something stupid like that?

I would.

Or someone like me.

Or lots of someones like me!

In 1989 fear and insanity were monetized.

Ten years earlier, April 1, 1979, the first illegal, unlicensed bungee jumps were taken by members of the Oxford Dangerous Sport Club from the eighty-meter-high Clifton Bridge in Bristol, England. Yes, ironically, this was, indeed, on April Fool's day.

It caught on.

People were doing it anyway (illegally from bridges and such); someone simply monetized it.

Bungee jumping is slightly more advanced and perhaps a little safer than Ngol, but it's just as scary. In our collective brilliance, we have turned this ancient and dangerous ritual into modern dangerous entertainment – for which people will gladly pay.

It crossed the mind of a man by the name of AJ Hackett (a New Zealand entrepreneur) that people might like to do this because people are crazy and better yet they have money to spend to be crazy, so he could charge money to give them the chance to do something they feared and could kill them, and do it safely.

I am an adrenaline junky. I see nothing wrong with that idea. In fact, I see everything right with that idea. Monetizing risk and fear and danger – and fun – why not? Better yet, why? To make money while serving people's desire for adventure.

Bungee jumping is an extreme sport; an adventure much more fun than the flight to Reno and a little safer than the ancient manhood-proving activity. Instead of using green vines, we attach giant rubber bands to our ankles or attach a harness in the center of our bodies so it is possible for jumpers to stay upright if they wish. Our goal is no longer to smack or brush the ground. Our goal is to have fun and what could be more fun than bouncing on the end of a big rubber band after plunging toward impending death on the jagged rocks or toward possible bodily damage on a stunt man airbag below?

We are, of course, more sophisticated than ancient tribes; therefore, instead of proving your courage, we do this simply to enjoy the thrill of an apparent last-second avoidance of a painful death. That is sophistication.

Why do human beings do that? Because it is inherent in many of us to take a risk; to enjoy the thrill of doing something most others won't do; to have an experience most others will never have – or even dare to have.

Or perhaps it is because we are, as a species, slightly insane.

Perhaps a little of both?

I am, therefore, a Bungee Jump Master – in Japan.

Why Japan? Because I already speak Japanese. Something I am already doing. I found that I like bungee jumping, which was already being done by others and had been for centuries.

I didn't learn Japanese to do business in Japan. I do business in Japan because I already knew Japanese – and for some reason, unknown to them or their ancestors, the Japanese people love bungee jumping.

I also enjoy taking adrenaline-producing risk. Not stupid risk, fun risk.

So I monetized what I was already doing (speaking Japanese) and enjoyed doing (riding adrenaline-producing thrill rides) and, voila… a bungee jumping business – in Japan.

So, now, I am a Japanese Bungee Jump Master.

In this capacity, my job is to connect my client to a big rubber band and help them leap into the void. These are people who think being pushed, from the top of an eight story building, and plummeting head first toward the unforgiving earth is a fun idea, and are willing to pay good money to do so.

Bungee Jump Masters are trained, qualified, and have the authority, to push these poor souls off the tower into the abyss.

Newbie jumpers are usually as frightened as they are eager. You have to help them to the edge and beyond. In Japan, the conversation goes something like this.

I say, "Ii desu ka?" meaning "Are you ready?"

They respond, "Uh" or "Hai," indicating their consent.

I then say, "Seguro?"

They again respond, "Uh" or "Hai," in assent.

For two years, I asked the one-word question, "Seguro?" thinking it was Japanese. "Seguro" does mean "are you sure?" But it's not Japanese – it's Spanish.

My clientele did not know, understand or care what I was saying. They would just nod vacantly and, staring into the abyss or with eyes squeezed tightly shut, leap voluntarily – or allow themselves to be pushed/assisted – to their apparent doom. On a weekend, I might assist 1300 people off the edge. At $30 a jump that is a lot of monetizing fear.

Why do people actually pay to have experiences like this? Because it's *fun*. We seem to enjoy scaring ourselves and will pay for the privilege. My friend Brad Barton says, "We like to enjoy ourselves half to death."

AJ Hackett monetized that human trait. He set it up so he could charge money for something that people were inclined to do anyway.

Taking the Leap

As I said, we'd serve upwards of 1300 customers on a weekend. During the week? Not so busy. On the slow days my brilliant mind wanders and wonders.

At the bottom of the bungee jump tower, for safety, there often is an air bag like the ones stunt men use in Hollywood. They are roughly twenty feet by thirty feet rectangle and about six feet high when inflated. In theory, a person could jump from the top of the tower, which was over seventy feet high, land on the airbag, and survive.

I am at the top of this eight story high tower on one of these slow days with lots of time to think. My brilliant mind begins to cook up an idea: "Could I jump from up here without a cord and be okay? Would it hurt?"

I was not quite crazy enough to do that, so I come up with what seemed to be a reasonable alternative to a free fall. I could jump with a cord and wait for the bouncing to stop. I would then be about fifty feet above the bag. There I could unhook myself and fall into the mat – and see how it feels. Fifty feet is a bit high, but it's significantly less than eight stories.

Sure! That would work. I could handle that. Yes, I'm pretty sure I could.

So, I jumped. When the bouncing stopped, I was hanging at the end of the cord that is connected to my harness with a carabiner. My weight wouldn't let me disconnect. I was lowered to the mat and I unhooked. I went back up the tower to try again, insanely determined to figure out how to pull off this crazy stunt.

My brilliant mind went back to work. I made two loops out of a strap that connects to the carabiner. That gave me two handles. I could jump, holding on to the handles. Then, when the bouncing stopped, I could just let go and fall into the air bag from a height that seems more reasonable; however, in this case, the operational word is not "reasonable" it is "risky."

Of course, I had no idea if I would be able to hold on during that initial bounce. I thought I could, but was not sure. I was okay with that insecurity until I was actually standing at the edge with multiple stories of empty space between me and the ground.

Now that scared person standing on the precipice is me. My self-talk goes something like this. "Are you ready?" "Uh huh." "Seguro?" "Uh huh." I jump.

What a rush! Obviously, I was able to hold on. Clearly, I did not die because I am writing this. I came out unscathed; however, it wasn't so great for the equipment.

In my brilliant mind, the wheels of imagination had not turned far enough. There I was, hanging at the end of a stretched out rubber band. What happens when you let go of a rubber band stretched out by a two-hundred-and-twenty-pound weight?

I let go, enjoyed a two second free-fall and hit the mat with a loud SLAP. The big rubber band shot up and BAM! It hit the tower with a resounding bang. Everybody came running over to see what broke and who died.

Brilliant? Crazy? You decide. A monetized mindset is a little of both. Willing to try new things even if there is risk – sometimes especially when there is a risk – just try it.

Human beings seem to have a built-in desire, sometimes a need, to take a risk. Risk isn't stupid; stupid risk is stupid. The desire to take a risk is natural, whether to prove one's manhood or just to see what it feels like to do something we've never done. We seem to be the only animal on the planet that is willing to risk everything for the sake of fun or adventure.

So, go ahead, venture into the unknown – see what there is to see. This willingness to take a risk is an important characteristic of a Monetized Mindset.

And that is why I am a Bungee Jump Master in Japan.

What do you like to do?
What do you need to do?
What are you already doing?

Let's monetize it… and *Monetize Your Mindset* while you are at it!

"If you can't stand up, stand out."

~ Mike Schlappi,
    Wheelchair Olympic Gold Medalist

Chapter Eleven ~
Who Does That?

My wife and I had a gift card for a gourmet hamburger place, so we decided to try it out. We were escorted to our booth by the hostess and the waitress soon arrived: "Hi, my name is VoNique. I will be taking care of you. Can I get you something to drink? We have Coke products, strawberry lemonade, flavored limeades…"

My wife said, "I will have water with lemon."

I drink Pepsi, not Coke, but they only served Coke products, so I thought I would be funny, "I don't want you to have to go next door and get me a Pepsi, so I will just have water with lemon as well."

The waitress laughed. A few minutes later, she brought us our water with lemon, took our order and left.

My wife and I sat back in idle chit-chat for a moment, then I noticed the waitress headed back our way. She had one hand behind her back and a big smile on her face.

"I have a surprise for you," she announced. With a flourish, she presented a large, Pepsi – from a different establishment! She had gone upstairs to the food court in the mall and got me what I wanted – a Pepsi.

Wow!

Who does that?

I asked my wife "I wonder if it will be on my bill?" After all, technically, I hadn't ordered it.

Hiroko said, "Of course it will."

But it was not.

When the waitress brought me the bill, the Pepsi was not included. *Who does that?* She not only made my day – she made my week, my month, my year. She made me want to serve better – *be better*.

Her over-the-top customer service, her thoughtful consideration, is something I will always remember. It was just a Pepsi; but, it wasn't just a Pepsi, it was a small, unexpected, special act of kindness – that meant a lot. It also taught me a lot.

She elevated my thoughts, my realization of what "business…" well, not just business… what "life" is all about and how simple it is to do more than your customers expect of you; to step up and stand out; to *be* more.

I wondered if this was something I would have done. I think not, but I will try to do better from now on!

It surprises me how deeply her simple act touched me. I kept thinking about it. Who does this kind of thing? Someone pretty special I think. What triggered that act of kindness? Who was she? What made her even think to do something like that?

So I went back and gave her a gift card – a small token of my appreciation. We connected on Facebook. I wanted to learn more of what triggered her act of kindness.

From our correspondence, I learned that she had been going through some personal difficulties. She and her husband had been trying to have a child for almost fifteen years. They were seeing fertility doctors and running all sorts of uncomfortable tests and procedures. They never had been able to find anything wrong. Recently, they had moved on to in-vitro fertilization (IVF) which is very expensive. She had to give herself several prescription injections daily for months – pretty painful stuff. Her hopes had risen and fallen; still, through it all, her thoughts were for her friends, customers, people like me who she didn't even know. Perhaps it is those who go through the tough stuff that make the best friends and even the best business people.

She did not even realize how special I thought her extra effort was. I also found out that her "extra effort" didn't stop there. She has also been known to sit with a customer that always came in alone, listened to her stories and made her feel special. That is outstanding personal service.

How many other hearts, beside mine, had she touched that day, that week, that year with her simple service-oriented, think-of-others attitude?

When asked why she does these things she answered, "I always try to treat everyone with kindness, even when there isn't an obvious benefit to me. My own trials have taught me that everyone else is fighting their own battles that I may know nothing about and that I should give others the benefit of the doubt every time."

My monetized mind goes to work (of course). This young couple could monetize their experience, their struggle, their success by helping others who are going through the same struggle that they went through. (Yes, they did ultimately have a baby. It's a girl!)

Maybe that's how I could return the favor. I could help them monetize their struggle and their ultimate success!

Who would do something like that? I mean, who would monetize their struggle? You, and me, and anyone who cares about others' struggles and challenges. After all, central to a monetized mindset – required for true financial security – is an attitude of service, of sharing, of going the extra mile, of helping others do what you do for yourself.

We are not alone on this planet. It is required of each of us to serve others, but it is not required of us to be poor as we do so. It is okay, admirable, even required, to profit – in order to help more effectively.

It's not that hard to stand up and stand out; you just have to be willing to just a little extra. I will be forever grateful for the lesson in service that was shared with me by this waitress. She could actually recognize this as an opportunity, and take the next step toward financial security by sharing her journey, her challenge, her solutions, her victory, with the millions of other parents who also want to have a child of their own.

By the way, I actually wanted a *diet* Pepsi – but I didn't have the heart to tell her ~ LOL!

"Our greatest glory is not in never falling, but in rising every time we fall."

~ Confucius

Chapter Twelve ~
Staying Power

Every Saturday of my young life I would watch cartoons for four hours, then go horseback riding with my friends. On Saturday mornings, and only on Saturday mornings, from about six o'clock until about ten o'clock we could watch cartoons. That was the only time cartoons were on television, and that was the only thing that would get me out of bed that early in the morning.

After four hours of "Flintstones," "Scooby Doo," "Bugs Bunny," "Foghorn Leghorn," a couple of my friends and I would saddle up the horses and take off on a Saturday adventure.

George was the name of the horse I rode when I was seven. He was a great horse, a brown quarter horse with a black mane and tail. He stood seventeen hands high. A "hand" is roughly the width of an average man's hand, four inches, officially. Seventeen hands is a pretty tall horse.

He was kind of a hand-me-down from my big brother. George was initially purchased as a roping horse for my brother, but he would toss his head every time my brother would throw the rope, and that cost my brother accuracy and time. So George did not work out as a roping horse, but he was a good riding horse and he was considered my horse – or at least the one I would ride.

I liked George. But he wasn't really my horse. He was a family horse. That wasn't good enough for me. I wanted him to be my very own horse.

"Dad, when is George going to be my horse?"

"What do you mean? George *is* your horse."

"Yeah, but when is he *really* going to be my horse?"

Dad thought for a few seconds, then said, "Okay, Bart, George will be your very own horse the day you can put the saddle on him all by yourself."

This was great news. I had seen Dad saddle a horse, so I knew I could and I would too, eventually. But "eventually" was too far away for a seven year old. I wanted George to be mine – now!

George was tied up in back waiting for Dad to saddle him. I ran to the kitchen table, grabbed one of the chairs, dragged it outside and stood it beside George. I dragged the saddle from the tack shed over to the chair. If you are visualizing an English saddle, you're probably thinking, "Sure, no problem." A seven-year-old could lift that.

But, no, this was a full size western roping saddle; thirty-five or forty pounds of awkward weight. At seven years old, I tipped the scale at about sixty pounds. The saddle was seventy percent of my body weight, but you could not convince me it could not be done. I lugged this monster saddle over to where the horse was standing, lifted it to the chair, got up on the chair, and... nothing.

I couldn't lift the saddle off the chair much less heave it onto George's back. That was not going to happen that day or any day in the near future.

Time passed. My desire to saddle George, and thereby claim him as my own, remained strong. My ability to do so would take some time but I knew I would get there because I watched my dad and others do it.

I got bigger, older, stronger. I remained focused, determined. I kept trying. Eventually, I was able to lift it waist high. Not good enough yet.

More time passed and I kept trying. I would brace it against George's side, attempting to push it up and over onto his back. George was no help. He was trying to cooperate, but in the wrong way. He would feel me push against him (as I tried to slide the saddle up onto his back) and he'd dutifully move over. That would cause me to lose my balance and down I, and the saddle, would go.

George would look back at me wondering why I was on the ground; however, he was too polite to ask.

Five years later, after a thousand attempts to saddle George, and a thousand failures, I finally succeeded! The saddle suddenly slipped right into place! I cinched up the saddle, then stepped back bursting with pride and excitement. I observed my handiwork for a moment, then ran off to find my dad to tell him the good news.

George was now mine!

Yes, he was mine … just in time for me to sell him and buy Buck, a wise, old and wonderful buckskin roping horse.

Why did I continue to try for five years? Why didn't I just give up? Because I knew it could be done.

I had seen my father, my brother, and many others saddle their horses. Therefore, logically, I knew I could do it too. I just needed to keep trying. Learn more. Get stronger. Get taller. And I did. And it was worth it.

Learning to *Monetize Your Mindset* is a similar process. Part of it is learning *how* to do it, part of it is knowing you *can* and *will* do it, and then growing into it. You see others do it, and you are pretty sure you can do it. I believed I could saddle my horse like my dad did. Eventually I could – and did.

Just like I developed the skill to saddle my horse, you can learn to *Monetize Your Mindset.* It takes time and effort and maybe some personal development, some learning and putting yourself around people who have a monetized mindset, but you can and, after reading this book, likely will begin to monetize specific skills and skillsets here and there.

Then you will start to think of doing it as a matter of course. You will begin to notice things you like to do, need to do, and are already doing, and habitually begin to think of ways to help others do the same in a way that you could get paid for doing it.

Monetizing your mindset takes the same kind of attention, time, growth, practice and patience as it took me to learn to saddle my horse, but don't worry, it won't take you as long as it took me to learn to saddle George!

Yes, there is some growing involved, but not five years' worth.

Well… sometimes…

The URL[3] BackToMyWeddingWeight.com sat unused for eight years until I found a weight loss system that really worked – for me. It was not about the ninety-day challenge of me dieting and exercising. Eight years is a long time, but it was constantly on my mind as I searched out a product, a system that would work, really work, for me and others like me.

Many might have given up and let that domain name go but I hoped I would eventually find what I was looking for. Eventually I did. And, because I was ready for the opportunity, I had the site up and running within a few days and immediately began profiting from the opportunity of helping others do what I was doing and achieving measurable results.

That's the thing. One of the significant elements of *Monetize Your Mindset* is being prepared for the opportunities when they come your way and taking those opportunities.

Some things happen slowly; other things happen much faster. When you find (or create) the right system or product, it may be only a matter of days or hours before you monetize it and start reaping the financial benefits. This will happen almost automatically when you have the right mindset.

You know you have a monetized mindset when you start thinking, "How will I monetize that?" A monetized mindset is a developed response reaction – based on a reflexive instinct to survive, then succeed.

This mindset is supported by being prepared mentally and somewhat financially. Abraham Lincoln said, "I will prepare and someday my chance will come." He did prepare. His chance did come. Because he was prepared, and because he had the right mindset, he became president of the United States of America and preserved the Union. Because he was ready, he became the Great Emancipator.

Like President Lincoln, I got ready. My chance came when I found a weight loss system that worked for me. I had researched these kinds of systems for eight years – that's a long

---

[3]   Universal Resource Locator

time. When I found the system that actually worked, for me, it was only a matter of days before I fleshed out the content of the BackToMyWeddingWeight.com website and started to reap the benefits of my monetized mindset.

I monetized a system someone else had created. I had purchased another's ideas and profited from it legitimately by promoting it as an element of my own business(es).

BackToMyWeddingWeight.com has empowered me to help many others move back to, or at least toward, their wedding weight and I've profited from doing so.

And that's the secret. Get ready. Be ready. Be aware and your chance will come.

I will help you take advantage of it. I will help you get ready. I will help you recognize your chance when it comes. I will help you develop the mindset that will begin to habitually, intuitively, instinctively recognize and *create* residual income-producing opportunities.

How? Simple. By owning this book, you qualify for a free gift that will help do for you what my father did for me – create and exercise a monetized mindset.

To get this gift go to BartMerrell.com/book-gift and follow the prompts. Get ready. Be ready. Be aware. Your chance will come. This gift will help you do just that.

As I said, some ideas take root slowly, some happen almost immediately. Taking the first commercial bungee jump to Japan happened pretty fast. I was prepared, the opportunity came my way and two months later I was in Japan pushing (I mean "assisting") people off an eight-story bungee jump tower.

You create a win for everyone when you *Monetize Your Mindset*. With whatever idea, tool, or system that helped you achieve your goals, you help others accomplish theirs. That is what monetizing your mindset is about: enhancing your income as you help others enhance their lives.

"You miss 100% of the shots you don't take."

~ Wayne Gretzky ~ Michael Scott

"Luck is what happens when preparation meets opportunity."

~ Seneca, Roman Philosopher

Chapter Thirteen ~
What's Luck Got to Do With It?

The idea that "luck is preparation meeting opportunity" has been around at least since the time of the Roman Empire – and ignored or not understood for even longer than that.

Most people tend to think that rich people got rich because they are lucky. The fact is, however, that even people who are born into money maintain or enhance financial security because they are prepared when opportunity happens. Prepared how? They are geared to recognize opportunity and are willing to take the risk necessary to capitalize on it.

What kind of "preparation" are we talking about here? They have developed their awareness of opportunity that is already around them and they are inclined to take action. Their natural human attraction to adventure and risk, and their inclination to monetize what they discover, is the core attitude or position required to build and maintain a reliable residual income. It is the essence of "luck."

Let's rephrase Seneca's declaration. *"Financial security, and it's attending residual income stream,* is what happens when preparation meets opportunity."

Opportunity does present itself often; but you don't have to wait. In fact, your monetized mind is always thinking of ways to *create* opportunity, especially considering what you already have. What do you like to do? What do you need to do? What are you already doing?

When preparedness (including the willingness to take a risk) meets opportunity (including the ability to create opportunity) luck happens; *residual income* happens; a residual income stream – that continues to flow with or without residual effort.

That's sounds pretty "lucky" right?

Missed Opportunity

What if you see an opportunity, but don't have the foggiest idea what to do with it? Do something anyway.

Billionaire entrepreneur, Richard Branson, gives this sound advice: "If you see an opportunity and you don't know how to do it, say 'yes' and figure out how to do it later."

In other words, do what I *didn't* do with Topgolf.

In the early summer of 1994, while I was in Japan working on the bungee jump system, I first discovered Topgolf.

What is Topgolf? It is a driving range. It's more than that, actually, especially in the United States. Here there are driving ranges, a plethora of games, sports bars, even nightclubs. The one near where I live has over two hundred television sets. These multi-million dollar venues attract non-golfers as well as golf enthusiasts.

The core attraction is, of course, golf; hence its name. They provide driving ranges where the ball automatically comes up out of the ground you can set on a tee or just hit it off the grass. You don't have to take time to bend down if you don't want to. You just hit the ball and another pops out. You like it either because (1) you are lazy or (2) you are trying to improve your drive and the consistency helps you focus on your swing.

In Japan when the balls came out of the ground you already teed up and ready to hit. You would purchase a card with a set number of balls on it, insert the card in a machine, then swing away until you run out of balls. Then you buy more.

Your pre-purchased tee-ups go pretty fast because you don't have to bend down and set the ball on the tee.

Have you been to one of these places? It's a sweet deal for everyone, fun for the golfer, profitable for the investor. Topgolf is a money machine.

Topgolf is amazing and fun for everyone. It's a great opportunity. These franchises were all over Japan. They had proven themselves to be highly profitable, but no one had taken them to America. Why not me?

This was a great idea. I was impressed. I thought about bringing it to America. I looked into it, thought about it. I didn't know for sure what to do, though. I was not ready for the opportunity, so I let it slip through my fingers.

Opportunities don't go away. They just go to someone else. For years, friend and fellow speaker, Bob Kittell has shared this important point with his audiences. He says, "Is there such a thing as a missed opportunity? Nope, someone else always picks up the ones you leave behind."

Opportunity was there, but I was not prepared to do anything about it, so I missed it. But someone else didn't miss it. Someone else – a lot of someone else's, picked up this opportunity and they have been rewarded quite handsomely for it. They are the "lucky" ones! These Topgolf systems are now everywhere.

Why did I miss this opportunity? Where did I go wrong? I wasn't lucky? No, I wasn't prepared. I wasn't prepared financially or mentally. Whatever I did, I wanted to do it just right and I figured I shouldn't do anything if I didn't know how to do everything exactly right from the start.

This is a classic blunder.

I should have followed Richard Branson's advice, which bears repeating: "If someone offers you an opportunity, and you're not sure you can do it, say 'yes' – then learn how to do it later."

I knew this was a great opportunity. I was in the right place (Japan) at the right time (when these businesses were popping up). I should have just said "yes" then figured out the details later. But I didn't.

Lesson learned.

One of the most important elements to monetizing your mindset is that you are mentally and emotionally prepared at all times to recognize opportunities for what they are when they come your way and do something about them – now. Worry about perfection later. This is how a monetized mindset reacts to opportunity. This is one fundamental reason you achieve financial security and eventually prosperity. You respond differently to opportunity than the average person. You become lucky!

As I am writing this, cryptocurrency and blockchain technology are the upcoming thing; heck, they are the *booming* thing. Bitcoin is hitting new highs on a daily, even hourly, basis. At this moment, it is worth twenty times what it was just a year ago. What will it become? Who knows.

Do I understand a lot about it? No. Am I involved? Yes. Am I researching and learning about it? Yes. What I do know is that I wish I would have jumped into this market a year ago, or, even better, eighteen months ago. However, as they say, "better late than never," right? Yes (as long as it is not too late, "it's never too late" does not always apply with regard to specific investments)!

I am currently profiting from the crypto world and I believe I will continue to do so as I learn more… or, perhaps, by the time you pick up this book this may be something of the past.

Either way, in the meantime, I will have taken advantage of other opportunities. Why? Because I have a monetized mindset. I am aware, constantly aware, of what is going, and I am constantly thinking and instinctively responding to opportunity. It is as if there is a subprogram running in the back of my computer brain constantly thinking about what I like to do, what I need to do, what I am already doing – and how I will (not how I *could* or *can*, but how I *will*) make money from that and create a system for others to follow, so they will profit from it too. I am aware, prepared – lucky.

Becoming financially secure is an attainable goal for just about everyone. It isn't a mystery, or shouldn't be. Get into the right frame of mind so that you see, recognize, understand, and are constantly aware of the myriad of opportunities all around you – and start thinking about how you can create opportunity as well. Get used to looking at most everything through the lens of "How can I make money doing this?"

Everyone can be lucky. Everyone should be lucky.

"Success is not final. Failure is not fatal. It is the courage to continue that counts."

~ Winston Churchill

Chapter Fourteen ~
Change is Constant

Things change. Deal with it. If you can't deal with it, accept it. If you can't accept it, move on anyway.

When I was eighteen years old I saw the movie, *Man Hunter*. This was the first in a series of several films that revolve around Hannibal Lecter novels. *Silence of the Lambs* was the remake of the movie, "Man Hunter".

I was intrigued and inspired. Right then and there I decided that I would be an FBI agent, working in the Behavioral Science Division, hunting down serial killers and bringing them to justice!

My dad had a friend who was a retired FBI agent. So Dad took me to see him to find out what it would take for me to become an agent. He said that the least competitive way to get accepted into the FBI was to study accounting. *Accounting?* That certainly didn't sound very exciting.

It did make sense, though. Most accountants don't have the risk-taking personality to be an FBI agent (which I do – in abundance – hence, the bungee jump), but the FBI does need accountants for white collar crimes.

Once you get hired by the FBI, they will move you around to different types of jobs to see what you are best at. You are able to apply for different positions that you want. When you land on what you are really good at, they tend to keep you there. I was not interested in accounting and I was not so great at it either, but getting the accounting degree was a way to get in. It would not limit me to white collar crime and if I could prove to them that I was good at tracking down bad guys, I would have a shot. So, even though I was not a big fan of accounting, I studied it anyway and graduated with minors in Spanish and Japanese.

Before my last semester I took a break and went to help my dad on the farm in southern New Mexico to help me improve my Spanish. On the farm I spoke mostly Spanish, which was also considered by the FBI as an important qualification for an agent.

I was working a lot, making good money (to this day, I don't know what "bad money" is) and in my small town there was no place to spend it, so I saved it.

I had a little extra money burning a hole in my pocket. There were several Customs and Border Patrol agents who had just had RK surgery done on their eyes with great success.

Radial Keratotomy (RK) is a surgical process, developed in 1974, designed to correct your vision. I had been wearing glasses from age six. I still remember the day I got glasses. It was a depressing. I didn't want to be called, "Four Eyes."

I was pretty sure it was the optometrist's fault. I swear that when I walked into his office I could see just fine. It wasn't until he made me look through that stupid device, you know the where the optometrist says, "Which is better one or two?" He took the device away from my eyes and everything was blurry. I think the machine ruined my vision. That's my memory, and I'm sticking to it.

At any rate, I decided that I didn't want to be Clark Kent, I wanted to be Superman. I was going be a cool FBI agent without glasses! I opted for the RK surgery.

The surgeon made sixteen cuts in each eye. The procedure was a success. My vision went from 20/200 in one eye and 20/160 in the other eye to nearly 20/20 respectively. Glasses gone! Awesome. I began the application process for the FBI.

I was immediately rejected.

In those days RK surgery was experimental surgery, which automatically disqualifies you from the FBI.

I was devastated! I was one semester away from graduating in that stupid accounting program that I hated (remember I had enrolled in accounting just to get into the FBI) and was no good at. If the class had the word "accounting" in the title I would get a B- or a C+ at best – no matter how hard I studied. Did I mention I hated accounting?

I finished the semester and graduated with a degree that I did not like, in a subject I was not good at, to get into a program I was immediately disqualified for.

Sometimes life just doesn't turn out like you want it to, no matter how badly you want it to. What do you do? Deal with it. If you can't deal with it, accept it. If you can't accept it, move on anyway.

I'd like to say I moved onward and upward, but I didn't. I moved onward and downward. Here I was, a college graduate, doing landscaping part-time for five dollars an hour. I actually liked it, but I wanted more money. Besides, I thought I should get a real job using my degree. The opportunity to create the first bungee jump in Japan came my way. I knew Japanese. I was a qualified accountant. I took the opportunity. And, as you know, I moved up in the world. *Eight stories* up in the world.

"I've come to believe that each of us has a personal calling that's as unique as a fingerprint – and that the best way to succeed is to discover what you love and then find a way to offer it to others in the form of service, working hard, and also allowing the energy of the universe to lead you."

~ Oprah Winfrey

Chapter Fifteen ~
Fatal Flight of the Jumpmaster

The power of persistence isn't just dogged, bullheaded stubbornness; it is developing or signing up for systems that work, like buying a franchise (or franchising your own process). You, innovate, yes, but first "go with what brung ya."

The key to your endeavor **is to honor the process;** follow the system, without fear, without falter, and without fail.

Bungee jumping is a risky business. It is an "extreme sport." If it's not done right, it could prove fatal.

The company that I represented, however, offered the safest bungee jump experience available on the market. The reason it was safe was because of the systems and safety checks they had in place. A proper system can make the difference between life and death. They followed that system faithfully...

Except once.

Every employee, from the cashier to jumpmaster, had a part in this system, in fact, most positions rotated so everyone understood not just their immediate part in the process but also how their roles interacted with each other. This assured safety for our team and a thrilling, safe experience for the customer.

It all begins with the cashier. The cashier's job is not just to take money at the gate, the cashier also weighs the customers and gives them a color (pink, blue, green or orange) and a number (1, 2, 3 or 4) on a little disc. These colors and numbers are vitally important.

The color represents the size of the cord. The number determines the height on the tower at which the cord is attached based on the customer's weight. As the customer moves through the process the color and number alerts the rest of the team as to the proper height and size of the bungee cord for that particular client.

The harnesses are similarly color-coded (pink, blue, green, and orange), coinciding with the diameter of the cords (small, medium, large and extra-large).

If an orange customer jumps with a pink cord attached, it would stretch too far, likely break, slamming them into the ground. If a pink customer jumps on an orange cord, the shock from reaching the end of a too-resistant cord would likely injure the customer.

It is the duty of a person designated as "controller" to put the correct color harness on the customer. The customer then begins the long journey up the eight flights of stairs.

At the top landing, the assistant jumpmaster checks the color and attaches the correct cord. The assistant jumpmaster then hands off the customer to the jumpmaster, calling out the number that was given to the customer by the cashier.

This number lets the jumpmaster know at which height to set the cord so the customer doesn't hit the ground.

The jumpmaster and assistant are also harnessed and attached to the tower so they don't inadvertently fall. This system is put in place, and religiously adhered to, as it keeps both employee and customer safe. It is, in fact, a matter of life and death to follow protocol. The system creates a safe and successful jump – creating an ever more popular sport.

Have you ever been to Disneyland or Disney World? You have seen how long lines can get when it gets busy. When a child gets scared and hesitates to get on a ride, it can slow everything down. It's the same with adults who are contemplating jumping head first into an eight-story freefall! It's a long way down, and people can freeze with fear. It sometimes takes a long time to "take the leap." A jumpmaster sometimes has to "assist" those who are hesitant.

One particularly busy day, the jumpmaster was having trouble with a particularly nervous customer. She was afraid to jump, but didn't want to give up. The line was backing up. A senior staff member who was, at that time, at the bottom of the tower performing the harnessing duty, the controller, hurried up the tower to help out.

In so doing, he violated an important safety rule. He inserted himself in the situation, contrary to protocol. Not only was he doing someone else's job, he didn't "tie off," meaning he didn't attach a safety cord to his own harness with a safety line. He probably didn't do it because there were only two lanyards available and the acting jumpmaster and assistant were using them.

He turned the girl around so she was looking at him instead of the ground seventy plus feet below. It might be easier for her to just fall backwards. It worked. She was still frightened, however, and reacted predictably. As she tipped over backwards, she panicked and grabbed the harnesser, pulling him off the tower with her.

He fell to his death.

If he had followed protocol, he would have been tied off with a safety line. In fact, he wouldn't have been up there at all. But he didn't follow the system – and it cost him his life.

How about you? Do you have a system for creating a better life financially? Are you following your system? If you don't have a system, would a system help you reach your financial goals? If you have a system, follow it. If you don't, it may well cost you your business or financial life.

"The difference between a successful person and others is not a lack of strength, not a lack of knowledge, but rather a lack in will."

~ Vince Lombardi

Chapter Sixteen ~
A Good Excuse is Not
an Oxymoron

While reading this book have a million excuses crossed your mind as to why you are not already financially secure? Do you have excuses as to why you haven't done what Bob or Brad or Thomas or Atsumi or I or a dozen others not mentioned in this book have done?

Are they good excuses, or are they bad excuses?

You've heard it before. "There are no good excuses." It slides trippingly off the tongue of motivational speakers, but it's not true.

There actually are "good excuses." There are also "bad excuses."

Excuses are essentially problem statements. They are called "excuses" because people use them to excuse themselves from responsibility, or blame, thereby also excusing themselves from gathering more information. They also use them to excuse themselves from doing or continuing to do something stupid or inefficient, so they don't keep doing dumb things.

Excuses, good or bad, are created by lack of information and what you do or don't do about that lack of information.

Good excuses are honest statements of difficulty, improbability, impracticality or, more rarely, impossibility. They are problem statements that, when honestly examined, produce real reasons for problems that prevent you from moving forward. They help you clarify the situation so you can gather more information that will help you move forward or intelligently change course.

Good excuses clarify situations in order for you to seek information that will help you make better decisions about how to move forward. *"Good excuses" is not an oxymoron.*

Bad excuses are based on faulty, inadequate, incomplete, even false information that leads you to walk away without trying. Bad excuses are, in effect, dishonest statements of difficulty when we accept them as final, insurmountable truths (that aren't really true) about impossible barriers (that really aren't impossible or, perhaps, aren't barriers at all). Bad excuses are used to justify giving up without getting more information that could help us succeed.

Bad excuses cause us to give up and watch the *Home Shopping Network* and spend money that we don't have instead of making money that we should have!

It is in your intention, not your situation, and the presence or absence of information that cause your success or failure. It is what we chose to *do* with an excuse that makes the excuse good or bad.

Psychiatrist Theodore Rubin said, "The problem is not that there are problems. The problem is expecting otherwise and thinking that having problems is a problem."

Most people really do think that having a problem is a problem. It's not true. Humans are made to solve problems. We actually invent problems for fun: checkers, chess, poker, football. We invent problems for the sole purpose of learning how to solve problems. What would happen if we did not have problems? We'd be bored stiff. We like to solve problems! Having a problem, therefore, is not the problem; thinking that having a problem is a problem – that's the problem.

Physicist Albert Einstein declared that "understanding the nature of the problem is halfway to the solution." He didn't say understanding the *problem* is halfway to the solution, he said understanding the *nature* of the problem is halfway there.

The problem may be obvious: *I don't have a website.* The nature of the problem is the "why" of it: *Why don't I have a website?* It is the "why" that leads us to the solution. What is the problem rooted and grounded in? What fruit does it produce? Good fruit? Bad fruit? Forbidden fruit? That's, "the nature of the problem."

Understanding the true nature of the problem puts you in position to solve it; to reframe the problem as goals and objectives that, with additional information and good planning, create success.

I don't promote my idea or project or business because I don't have a website.

It's probably true that a website would help you promote your business, so the statement is a problem statement about why you feel stuck. When you use that statement to give up without trying, it's a *bad* excuse. When you use it to move forward and learn how to create a website or find someone to build it for you it is a *good* excuse.

I don't know how to build a website or get one built.

That's a bad excuse unless you are saying it so you can figure out what it takes and set a goal in place so you can get one built. Then it's a good excuse because a good excuse identifies what is truly needed to reach your goal.

An excuse is only a bad excuse when you use it as a justification for giving up. Especially when more information would reveal that you don't have to give up and that to continue might be worth the effort.

Remember, the word "excuse" actually means to excuse yourself from fault or simply excuse yourself from moving forward. Sometimes that's a good idea, sometimes it is not.

If excusing yourself from moving ahead on your plan is based on inadequate or poor information, and you won't examine the facts further for real causes that can be solved, it is a bad excuse. If excusing yourself from moving forward is based on a thorough examination of the facts, including the effort or costs required to move forward, measured against a realization that there are inadequate or diminishing returns that make the effort not worthwhile, it's a good excuse.

I don't know how to do this, so I'll give up now (bad excuse).

I don't know how to do this, so I'll find out how (good excuse).

I found out how to do this, but it's not worth the effort, so forget it (good excuse).

It has everything to do with focus. When Michael Jordan brought the ball down the court on a successful fast break, what do you suppose his focus was on? Putting the ball in the hoop. Yes, the obstacles, the opposing players, were important, but they were in his peripherals. If they were his focus instead of the goal. he would never have scored, certainly not enough to be an icon in the world of sports.

The important thing, then, is to focus on the goal and keep the problems in your peripherals. Seek out mentors and coaches who share that same focus, who have accomplished what you are trying to accomplish: keeping clearly in mind what you want, not what you don't want, and why things will work, not why they won't.

Yes, good coaches bring up practical issues and valid concerns, but their focus, and yours, is on the why *to*, not the why *not to* – the why it *will* work, not the why it *won't* work.

What if Bill Gates or Steve Jobs had bad coaches or listened to their detractors? What would the world look like today? What if Michael Jordan listened to his high school coach, the one that cut him his sophomore year? "MJ" would have a totally different meaning – or no meaning at all.

I don't have time.

That is one of my favorite excuses. Is it yours?

It might be considered a bad excuse because it's really not true. Everyone has the same amount of time in a day, so it's not a question of time; it's a question of priorities. It may, however, be considered a good excuse if you use it as a wake-up call to re-examine your priorities and organize your time better.

Fellow speaker, Trapper Woods, created an unusually effective time management program and had it published. The day before he was scheduled to launch the program, he found a misspelled word. He was frustrated because he didn't feel right about marketing an "imperfect" program.

His wife, Brenda, also his business partner, suggested that he just tell his audience that there is a misspelled word in his program, and the first one to find it would get a free system. It would be fun and would get people to review the program more thoroughly at the event.

It worked. People immediately began to comb through the program looking for the misspelled word. In the process, they discovered how good the program really was.

It worked too well.

When they returned from their break, sure enough, the misspelled word had been found. He gave the lucky participant the (rather pricey) program – then another hand went up.

"How about *this* misspelled word?"

Different audience members had found six misspelled words. Trapper had to give away six programs, not just one.

It turned out to be a great deal, for his audience. It also turned out to be a good deal for him. He sold a whole lot more programs than he would have without the mistake because his audience went through the program and loved what he had it!

What a great lesson in going ahead and doing something, even if it isn't perfect.

My second biggest excuse is the brother of perfection. It is what I call perfect procrastination. I procrastinate doing something or completing a project or publishing something (like this book) because I don't think it is perfect enough.

"If you want to influence the least amount of people ever, wait until it is perfect." Wise words from my friend and mentor Ray Higdon.

What if the book is flawed because there may be misspelled words or grammatical errors? "I can't publish this book until it's perfect."

Perfect procrastination is a huge obstacle for many of us.

"Courage to me is doing something daring, no matter how afraid, insecure, intimidated, alone, unworthy, incapable, ridiculed or whatever other paralyzing emotion you might feel. Courage is taking action, no matter what. So you're afraid? Be afraid. Be scared silly to the point you're trembling and nauseous, but do it anyway!" [Richelle E. Goodrich]

One of the biggest causes of perfect procrastination is fear of what people will say. Will they laugh at me? Hate on me? Maybe they will call me names! "Sticks and stones will break your bones but names will never hurt you," is simply not true. Criticism and rejection, especially from friends and family, may hurt, but it is not fatal – unless you let it be.

In fact, taken with the right attitude, criticism can be helpful. Receive it, look at it, glean anything helpful from it then let go of it. It might be helpful to realize that even the most beautiful song on YouTube will have many thumbs down (dislikes). Even the best speeches will have dislikes. The greatest story will leave someone saying, "Bo-o-o-r-ing."

Criticism is inevitable. Expect it, look at it, gain whatever bits of help it can lend you – then let it go.

Your biggest critic, by the way, is generally you. It is usually in your own head. This critic you can control. Put a muzzle on this critic. Self-criticism is entirely self-defeating and stops you from influencing people.

The truth is that truth is your biggest ally. Be aware. Know your strengths. Know your weaknesses. Get out there, hustle and make things happen. And when the critics do what critics do, first consider what they have to say, then, if it doesn't apply ignore them.

"Two roads diverged in a wood, and I – I took the one less traveled by... and that has made all the difference." [Robert Frost 1874-1863]

When two roads diverge in my woods. I also tend to take the one less traveled. That's why I've never had a real job – and I am glad I haven't. The tendency to take the road less traveled also brings me face to face, quite often in fact, with the question, "When is enough, enough? When do I quit? When do I holler 'Uncle'"?

How about you? Do you travel the untrammeled path? How far you do go down that road less traveled? Do you ever turn around and go back? If so, when – or why? When do you know when it's time to quit? That's the question.

The answer is, "It depends." (How's that for raw brilliance?)

There are two games I very much enjoy playing: poker and chess. I've played them so long I don't even remember learning how to play. My two older brothers-in-law told me they taught me when I was three or four years old. I was so young it just seems like I have always known how to play. Poker is my favorite. I love the math, the statistics, the mental strategies inside the game. It is fun.

A few years ago, I found out you could play poker online for money. So I started playing for very low stakes online – dime and quarter stakes. It's called "low stakes poker". Soon I was playing in small, friendly local games. I did well. I thought perhaps I could be a professional poker player. I loved the adrenaline rush.

I consumed textbooks on poker psychology and poker strategy. The crazy thing was how much I enjoyed studying the game. It didn't feel like studying – certainly nothing like studying accounting in college. Perhaps that was because one was passive math and the other was more active, exciting, fun math. Accounting math *reported* [accounted] for what happened, poker math *caused* things to happen. There was great potential for gain – with a risk of disaster!

I actually became quite good. I am what is referred to as a "tight" player. That means that while I do have the guts to push all in, I don't take stupid risks. Most of the times when I pushed I had the "nuts" (the best possible hand at the time). I played poker eight to ten hours a day.

I was mainly an online tournament player. It would cost ten to one hundred dollar to enter a tournament; there would be four to ten thousand players at the start, and it would take two to five hours to finish if I played well. If not, it would be over in five or ten minutes.

My best finish was second place. It was a ten dollar buy-in and it took just under four hours to finish. I won $2,700. Not bad for a few hours work – or play. Like I said, I was a pretty good poker player and I certainly did enjoy it. So why am I still not playing?

It wasn't worth my time.

I wasn't losing money, but I wasn't making much either. After eight months of playing eight to ten hours a day my poker account was $560 net positive. Do the math. Eight months at roughly eight hours a day seven days a week is 1,920 hours. $560, therefore, represented earnings of twenty-nine cents an hour for my time. The ROI was just not there. It was fun, therefore not really a waste of time, but it wasn't quite fun enough to justify the time invested. So I quit. Well, I put it on the back burner, at least. Maybe someday…

How about you? When is enough, enough – for you? When and how do you decide when to stay and fight or throw in the towel? Do you quit for good or just adjust your priorities and put in on the back burner?

Again, that depends. How bad do you want whatever it is you are after? It also depends on the potential benefit. What is the potential benefit? Is that a likely benefit? What is – or could be – the cost? Is what you are doing putting you in any mental, physical, financial or emotional peril? How about the people around you: your family, your employees, those who depend on you? Are you willing to pay the price to make it happen, whatever that price may be? Is that an acceptable or unacceptable risk for you and the people around you?

Remember George the horse? It took five long years before I was able to put the saddle on by myself and claim ownership. Why didn't I quit? I invested seven times the time in George the horse, who I loved, more than I did in poker, which I also loved. Why? Was that reasonable?

What it is you are trying to accomplish? What is a reasonable expectation for its accomplishment? How much time? Effort? Money? What is reasonable – to you? What is reasonable to a professional or an expert in the field? Who have you consulted with – other than your cousin, Jethro, who has an opinion about everything? Do you have a mentor, someone who is accomplished in the field?

Was it reasonable of me to think eight months was enough time to become a professional poker player? Probably not, but it was all I was willing to give at the time. George was different. I knew I needed to get bigger, stronger. I knew it would take time, but I also knew for certain that it would happen. This particular investment of time had a guaranteed eventual outcome that would assure success.

Not so with poker. I was not willing to put in the time and the effort to advance my skills enough get to a point where I could play poker at a better rate of return than twenty-nine cents an hour (Remember, poker is *not* a game of chance, it is a game of skill and strategy. You earn what you win; you win what you earn).

However, playing in the World Series of Poker is still on my bucket list. So when the situation changes or when I have nothing better to do, I'm going for it!

What is the norm for what *you* are trying to accomplish?

Here is another factor for consideration. Are you on the upside or the downside of a trend? You just opened a franchise. It cost you $500,000 to open. How long do you give it before you close it down? What is the industry average? Three years? Five? Is the franchise trending on getting more popular or less popular? All of these questions must be answered, or at least considered. All impact your decision.

Is there any tangible, relevant evidence that suggests that you are succeeding and you should keep going?

Here is another question, one you need to consider carefully. What about your "sunk cost," the $500,000 investment (to say nothing of your time). You can't recover it until you make a sufficient profit. Some people hold on too long because they can't let that go. "I've invested this much; I just can't turn my back on it."

Generally, this is not a good position from which to make that kind of decision. It's the classic, "Don't throw good money after bad."

If your franchise as a whole is trending up, it might be a valid decision to hang on and even invest more. But if it is trending down in popularity and the downward trend has no end in sight, it's probably a good decision to let go of your sunk costs. Don't let "sunk costs" sink you.

This is a perfect example of when a good excuse really is a good reason to change direction, change strategy, sell out, or simply stop. You are making a new decision based on current or reasonably projected information or circumstances. You are not giving up or giving in because you're a quitter.

"Two roads diverge in the woods…" and you decide to take the one less traveled. "How far do you go down that road?" That becomes the question.

And still the answer is? "It depends."

What if you really mess up? "Love yourself. Forgive yourself. Be true to yourself. How you treat yourself sets the standard for how others will treat you." [Steve Maraboli]

"Letting go means to come to the realization that some people are a part of your history, but not a part of your destiny." [Steve Maraboli]

Surround yourself with like-minded people. People that support and encourage you. My dad encouraged me from a very young age. That is why I am the way I am, why I have a *monetized mindset.*

Remember Brad, my friend who made money from honey? When I asked him what made the difference between it being a hobby (not making money) to it becoming a business (making money), he said in effect, "It was hanging out with people who have monetized mindsets."

My editor, who happens to be very good at what he does professionally, has said many times as we have been writing this book together that he has gained many insights from the experience and just being around me. I asked him how.

"This book isn't just about financial security," Thomas said. "This is about hope. You, your concept, this book, instills hope – not just for me but for everyone I care about. You create genuine hope that we really can all be financially secure, and that we can all be in a position do deal with what happens when whatever happens, happens," He said, "Bart, do you even get the power of your own message?"

I hope so.

"When you take risks you learn that there will be times when you succeed and there will be times when you fail, and both are equally important."

~ Ellen DeGeneres, *Seriously ... I'm Kidding*

Chapter Seventeen ~
Just a Journal

Have you ever given it your all and still come up short? In the movie, *A Knight's Tale*, the good guy suffers a significant (though temporary) setback. He is approached by the sneering, gloating villain, who says, "You have been weighed, you have been measured, and you have been found wanting."

A while ago, I enrolled in an online course about online marketing. After our first week of training we had a contest. The top three in the contest would win an Italian leather-bound journal.

It was an exercise. It involved creating something and putting it out there whether or not it was perfect, just to see how it was done. You were to actually do something, to learn, experientially. You were to create a short two to three minute video that shared one of the ideas you got from the class so far, post it to a site, then share the link with as many people as you could think of, and ask them to take action which, in this case, was to simply click "vote". This really only verified that they got it, thereby giving you your score.

It didn't matter how perfect your message or idea on the video was or what quality of camera work was involved. It was an exercise to get you to actually *do* something, whether it was perfect or not, to get people to act (vote) in much the same way you might try to get people to buy something.

The three students that generated the most votes would win a beautiful Italian leather journal.

I decided that I was going to win the contest – or at least be in the top three.

It wasn't just about the journal; it was about winning. I've always been competitive. In high school, I had several opportunities to take part in similar contests, mostly – FFA [Future Farmers of America] fundraisers. I won every contest I entered.

One of these activities involved selling boxes of oranges. Whoever sold five hundred dollars' worth or more would win a pair of Justin Roper Boots. As I recall, I was the only one who hit the five hundred dollar mark. I actually exceeded it; doubled it. I sold over $1100 worth so I asked for two pair; one for me and one for my girlfriend.

When the boots arrived she was no longer my girlfriend. She gave them to her sister-in-law. The boots didn't matter. Maybe the girlfriend didn't either, I don't know. I do know one thing: winning mattered.

Another fund-raiser involved selling magazines. Points were given for every subscription sold. You used the points to buy things out of a catalog. Thumbing through the catalogue I spied a .243 rifle. That's what I wanted! (I'm fairly certain I could not win a firearm in a high school contest today!)

Not only did I earn enough points for my rifle but I exceeded it. I gave my extra points away to friends to help them get what they were shooting for (no pun intended).

Now I had my sights set on the Italian leather journal. It wasn't that the journal was so important – you could buy one on Amazon for maybe eighty bucks – I just wanted to win. There were over one hundred and twenty participants. I made my video, started promoting it and counting the number of hits.

Votes could not be repeated for the same person. The understanding was that your people could only vote for you once. The system was set up to accept only one vote from each IP address for each contestant, forcing us to expand our markets.

I watched the vote count closely. If anyone was getting close, I would enhance my efforts. I tried to stay ahead, gain some cushion between the other participants and me. I was willing to do most anything to win – even going house to house in my neighborhood to gather votes.

I woke up the morning of the last day of the contest in third place with a ninety-point lead over fourth place. I might not win, but confident I would be in the top three. I had it in the bag. Like me, everyone else must also be running low on people to contact and ask for a vote.

I check the vote count again thirty minutes later. I was stunned to see that I was now in fourth place. Someone not even on my radar had blown right by me! My comfortable lead had vanished. I was now down by over two hundred and fifty votes. In minutes, even as I watched, I dropped to fifth place. First, second, third, and now fourth place were two hundred fifty to three hundred votes ahead of me.

How could this happen? How could it happen so fast? There was no way I could make up that kind of ground. I had two hundred and eighty-four votes and it had taken me over four days to get those. There was no way I could get another two hundred and fifty plus votes by the close of the contest.

I had done all I could – and failed. I had been weighed, I had been measured, and I had been found wanting. It was depressing. How could I lose? I never lost if I committed to it!

I sat in front of my computer, feeling sorry for myself. I tried to figure out how they were able to jump past me so quickly. I'm not sure what possessed me to think of this, but I did a Google search on "contests" and "votes." You will never guess what came up… You can buy three hundred votes for twenty bucks.

Now not only was I dealing with the fact that I did all I could and came up short. Now I had to consider that people were beating me by cheating.

I was disappointed… upset… I was angry.

But it was just a journal, right?

I talked to a friend about it and he suggested that I do the same thing. Buy votes. It seemed like a good idea. I gave it some thought, but it didn't seem right. Even if technically it wasn't against the rules, it didn't support the intent of the contest, and I knew it. If I ended up getting the journal that way, I would not gain the sense of accomplishment of winning in a way that seemed fair and square.

This was not about the journal at all.

No, I didn't buy votes. I finished in fifth place. Yes, I was disappointed. But I learned three things about myself that made it worth the effort – kind of (I was still disappointed).

The first thing I realized was that I can give it my all, fall short and be okay with that, as long as I do my best.

The second thing was that I am willing to play until the end of the game, even when it seems hopeless.

The third thing was that even when things are not fair, I am able to stick to my sense of fair play – my integrity and that is what is important.

"To be independent of public opinion is the first formal condition of achieving anything great." [Georg Wilhelm Friedrich Hegel]

A few hours later, the teacher posted a video saying that there were some anomalies in the voting, so the leader board had been taken down while they sorted things out. The winners would be announced at the beginning of the webinar Monday evening. That was three days away. I did not want to wait three days for this to get sorted out!

I know, I know; it was just a journal.

Monday evening finally arrived. The instructor revealed how some contestants had bought votes and, while he had not said, specifically, it was against the rules; he also said that he should not have had to.

"And the winners are…" A picture of the first place winner appeared on the screen.

It was me! I WON!

I had been elevated from fifth to first place! All of those in front of me had purchased votes.

I jumped up, ran into the other room where my wife was sitting quietly minding her own business (she knew what was going on with the contest and that I was losing and how I felt about it all).

I was jumping up and down like a kid on Christmas morning, "Hiroko! Whose husband is a winner?"

She looked up at me with no expression whatever. I repeated it insistently, *"Whose husband is a winner?"*

"You are."

"No, *your husband* is a winner."

I must have done this ten times a day for a week. "Hiroko, whose husband is a winner?" Eventually she just said "Yeah, yeah, I know my husband is a winner." I'm surprised she didn't start giving me doggie treats!

It wasn't just a journal. It was an important learning experience. The first thing I learned is that it's okay to take a risk of failing and, if I do fail, I must be okay with that as long as I do my best and learn something in the process. The second thing is to play until the end of the game, even if it seems hopeless. The third thing is that even when things don't seem fair, stick to your sense of fair play, your integrity, and, who knows, it might all work out after all – or not – but either way, you are okay.

In this case, I held to my integrity and was ultimately rewarded.

This journal now has an honored place in my office.

It is much more than just a journal.

"It is better to fail and be disappointed than to not try and always wonder, What if..."

~ Bart Merrell

Chapter Eighteen ~ Acres of Pig Poop

Remember the story, Acres of Diamonds? [4]

Ali Hafed sold his farm and went in search of diamonds. He died poor, alone, in a foreign land. He never found his riches. The people that bought his farm however, discovered diamonds! Lots of diamonds. Literally acres of diamonds. The most magnificent diamond mine in the world, the Golconda mine, was established right there in what was once Ali Hafed's backyard.

My family has a similar story. Instead of "Acres of Diamonds", I call it "Acres of Pig Poop".

I grew up in a small town in southern New Mexico. There were more pigs than people in my town. We had roughly eighteen thousand pigs at any given time. That creates a lot of pig poop.

We built three man-made ponds called the lagoons that we would divert the pig poop. It would decompose, evaporating off the water and methane gas and, eventually, the stink.

We would fill one pond, move to the next, then to the next, and then come back to the first pond and begin the cycle over again. You did not want to live downwind of our property.

My dad was not only a farmer, he was a businessman. He enjoyed creating ways of making money. This was a profitable operation, but wasn't enough for my entrepreneur-minded father.

In his late sixties, he shut down the pig operation and started looking for new opportunities. He died at age eighty-one without finding his next acres of diamonds.

A few years after his death we sold the farm for $235,000 – a fair price for the property.

---

[4]   https://en.wikipedia.org/wiki/Russell_Conwell

A few months later, the new owners were leveling the lagoons. The ground was dry on top, but the heavy grader broke through the crust and sank to its belly in black muck.

Worried, they called in experts to take a look. The experts analyzed the stuff and offered the new owners two thousand dollars a ton.

That is a dollar a pound for old pig poop!

There was over five hundred tons of the stuff. In his search outward, Dad had overlooked the inherent value of old pig poop as one of the richest sources of fertilizer on the planet. The farm that we sold for $235,000 was suddenly worth over one million dollars.

Five hundred tons of yucky old pig poop was, literally, acres of diamonds right under Dad's nose.

Where are your acres of diamonds? Are they right under your nose? Where is the real smell of success? Does it smell like money? Roses? Pig poop?

Is there something you are overlooking? Maybe an unpleasant experience or situation that you overcame for yourself, and could help others do the same. Or some skill that has helped you through a tough situation like it did for Thomas or Bob, or something fun that could be a family business like Brad's Bees.

What is it you like to do, need to do, or are already doing that you could monetize? And, in the process, could you teach others to monetize their mindset for themselves or teach other professionals to do for others and get paid for it?

Don't overlook your acres of diamonds as did Ali Hafed and my dad. Awareness is key to monetizing your mindset.

> *What do you like to do?*
> *What do you need to do?*
> *What are you already doing?*

> *Let's monetize it!*

"Vision without action is merely a dream. Action without vision just passes the time. Vision with action can change the world."

~Joel A. Barker

Epilogue ~
What Now?

Now that you've finished reading the book, it is time to devolve into some shameless self-promotion, not shameless promotion of me and what I can do for you. No, I mean shameless promotion of *you* and what you do for others, your dreams, your desires, your passions, and start making money doing it.

Most great speeches, books, articles, sermons end with a call to act. So here's the call to act for your newly monetized mindset: Act!

That's it. Do something. Try something. Monetize something. See how it works. If it doesn't work, that's okay, try something else. Try, try again, and have fun doing it.

If you are an employee and get a W-2 every year and you don't have a side hustle (a side business) you need to get one. The tax benefits alone are worth it (check with your accountant about this).

So…

What do you *like* to do?

What do you *need* to do?

What you are *already* doing?

It is *time* to monetize it!

Grab a notepad, turn on your computer, grab your cellphone or whatever it is you use to make lists. List all the things you like to do, need to do and are already doing. Pay special attention to things you do regularly.

Continually grow that list by constantly writing down all the things that occur to you, even if you don't know yet, or for sure, how to monetize them.

Don't be limited by practicalities, at least not yet, just consider possibilities. Don't even trouble yourself with the "how" just get imaginative about the "what."

In fact, it would be premature for you to immediately concern yourself with exactly *how* you are going to profit from your ideas, just get them on paper (or in your computer) or whatever way that works for you to keep track of your ideas and keep them in the forefront of your mind.

Stay open. Wonder "what" and "what if" but don't worry about "how." Bob Proctor suggests that "If you [already] know what to do to reach your goal, it's not a big enough goal."

Paraphrasing Mike Rayburn in his book *What if...?* When you say to yourself or someone else says to you, "You can't do that."

Just say "Yeah, I know, but what if I could? How would I start?" That question leaves the possibilities open.

Building this list of possibilities is the first step in monetizing what you like to do, need to do or are simply doing already. While it may be true that you can't do everything right now, you can certainly start *thinking* about everything right now.

This is not about the short game. This is about the long game. It's not about getting rich quick – or slow. It may not be about getting rich at all. It's about building financial security by identifying and taking advantage of opportunities that are all around you.

So do it. Start your list now. Consider every possibility. Have fun with this. Ideas beget ideas – and more ideas. Even seemingly ridiculous ideas sometimes turn out to be profitable. Remember the Pet Rock? The Big Mouth Billy Bass singing stuffed fish? Billy Bob Big Cletus Snaggle Biker Teeth? These crazy ideas made millions! Look back to the different side hustles from this book. Do they spark any ideas for you?

Sometimes a great idea turns out to be an unworkable idea, which then evolves into a better idea which is marketable – until the market changes or a better idea comes along. Then, once again, it's outdated or superseded. Then a new idea comes along – horse and buggy is replaced by the automobile, fax machine is replaced by email, Blockbuster is replaced by Redbox rentals, Redbox is challenged by streaming videos online.

The goal is that the next innovative money-making idea that comes along is *your* idea.

As long as you stay open and aware, always adding to your list of possibilities, you will succeed; maybe not immediately, but ultimately you will.

BackToMyWeddingWeight.com was on my list for eight years before it materialized into an income stream. Taking the first commercial bungee jump to Japan was not on my list at all, but I've always been an adrenaline junkie and when the opportunity came up to monetize that particular addiction by building bungee jumps, I jumped at the chance (pun intended). I was soon on my way to Japan to help push (I mean "assist") people jumping off bungee towers that I helped build.

Some things may indeed happen quickly, like my work on the bungee towers in Japan. I recognized that opportunity immediately because (1) I enjoy taking those kinds of risks and (2) I spoke fluent Japanese, so it was an obvious fit and an immediate success.

Other things take years to develop, but develop they do. You don't have to do everything at once – just start now and do something.

Here is the short list of what we will do right now:
- Build your list of possibilities.
- Establish a contact list.
- Purchase relevant domain names.
- Set up your social media profiles.
- Set up a Facebook Fan Page.
- Set up a blog website.
- Create content.
- Engage your Tribe – re-engage it – and re-engage it...
- Engage your market again.

Let's look at each of these in more depth.

Build a list of possibilities and contacts. In most cases, you want to build a list of potential clients. Create your following, your tribe, people who are interested in you and what you have to offer. Collect names and email addresses. Perhaps their phone numbers (at the time of this writing text marketing is big). In time this may change. The tactics and methodology may change; however, the goal will remain. *Be the one people think of when they need your kind of service.*

Purchase a domain name. Go to GoDaddy.com or another domain retailer on line or call them. First, see if your name is available. If it is, buy it, no matter what. You will be glad you did – unless you change your name. If someone has "[your name].com," pout for a second, then let it go, for now, and focus on other options.

I don't recommend using your name with a .net or a .biz or .org because people tend to automatically use .com and you'll be sending them to someone else's site.

Also you if your name is often misspelled it is a good idea to buy the misspelling .com if it is available. For example, my name Bart Merrell is often spelled "Bart Merrill". Bart*Merrill*.com was available and on the advice of one of my mentors, Heather Lutze, author of *Marketing Espionage,* I purchased that misspelled domain and pointed it to the correctly spelled BartMerrell.com. If you go to Bart*Merrill*.com it will automatically pull up BartMerrell.com.

I own BartMerrell.com and BartMerrill.com. I also own NeverHadARealJob.com, BackToMyWeddingWeight.com, 500dollarcashflow.com and MonetizeYourMindset.com (I was surprised and lucky that it was still available). At the time of this writing, I am using BartMerrell.com and BackToMyWeddingWeight.com and am building MonetizeYourMindset.com. I have tentative plans for the others and paying the annual fee to keep them, for a while at least, is a reasonable investment.

Set up a Facebook Fan Page and Facebook Group. Set up the page with the same name as your .com domain name. Lock up the same name(s) by doing the same thing in all of the different social media mediums that you may eventually use (Facebook, Twitter, LinkedIn, etc. wherever your clients hang out, where you will be able to interact with them and draw them to you). Again, the type of social media and the tactics used on these mediums may change, but your goal is still the same – to create name recognition and be the "go to" person for whatever it is you offer. This universal advertising/marketing principle was valid long before texting and social media and it will be valid when the next thing comes along too. Be the first one someone thinks of when they need what you have to offer.

Set up a blog/website. If you can't build one yourself and you can't yet afford to have someone do it for you, start with your Facebook fan page.

If you have any questions about how to do this, go to BartMerrell.com and click on "find out how."

Create content. Offer value. Teach people something, something they can use. Inspire them to do better, be better. Tell stories. Be interesting. Be concise. It is said that a goldfish has a twelve-second attention span. It is also said that the average person's attention span today is shorter than that of a goldfish. Currently ours is eight seconds – down from twelve seconds a few years ago! So you have eight seconds to catch your potential client's attention – or "poof" they are gone.

Engage your Tribe. Even with all these things in place you have to market yourself or pay someone to do it for you. In the social media world, that requires engagement. In social media, the operational word is "social." You must get social. Communicate with your audience. Get noticed. Stand out.

Remember VoNique, the waitress that brought me my Pepsi? Be like her. Do *something* different – not just *anything* different – something that makes a positive or constructive difference, something that catches people's attention, something that makes them want to come back to you for whatever else you have to offer. Go the extra mile – heck, just go the extra half a mile and you will be further ahead than most.

Your content needs to be good, helpful, competent, but it doesn't need to be perfect. (Remember the problem of "perfect procrastination"?) It needs to be authentic. You need to connect with your audience. It is not your job to decide if it is good enough. Yes, do your best but get it out there and let the market decide how good it is.

Engage your tribe again. Do this consistently, constantly. This will keep you in the front of your future client's mind. When they are in need of your services, they will think of you. Do this repeatedly. You will get better and better at it and will start to see results.

When it comes to content there are several options. Figure out what best suits you. Video (a YouTube channel or Facebook Live) is the way to go, at least at the time of this writing. But if creating videos freaks you out then create an audio recording (like a podcast). If that is too stressful for you, you still have the written word (written blog). Some people prefer that anyway. That's okay. You decide what might work for you, then *try it.* Do something. Try something. Be interesting. If it doesn't work, or you just don't know how, try something else. Try, try again – and have fun doing it. (again, if you have any questions or I can be of help with any of this, connect with me at BartMerrell.com).

Think "content, content, content." Be a "go to" person – the expert for your audience on whatever you offer.

To help build your list, your audience, find or create a reward, something to give people for putting in their name and email address. A giveaway like this is called "click bait".

At the writing of this book my giveaway is a Wealth Potential Analysis. It is a quiz to determine what your chances are of attaining financial security.

Go to BartMerrell.com, take the quiz and look at the other premiums. Now think about what kinds of giveaways would interest your ideal client, your audience, your tribe. What would be a good giveaway for you? What would attract your clients?

When they put in their info you will need a place for it to go, a CRM [Customer Relationship Management] auto-responder. They are free or require a small fee to manage your list. The company I started with charged me fifteen bucks a month to manage a thousand names/emails a month.

There are many to choose from: MailChimp, GetResponse, Constant Contact, AWeber. They are designed to help you keep in contact with your tribe with blogs, newsletters, etc. (with continually updated and new content) that alert your tribe to new – or additional – ideas related to you or your subject, product, service.

Does this make sense? Do you see how to do this? Start with the first bullet point and try it. Try everything until you run into something that you don't understand or don't know how to do, connect with me at BartMerrell.com, click on "learn more" and I'll help you.

Henry David Thoreau said that most of us lead lives of quiet desperation. It's true. But do we have to be "most people?" Do our friends have to be "most people"?

Strong, passive residual income is the goal – the Holy Grail of financial security.

What do you *like* to do?
    What do you *need* to do?
        What are you *already* doing?

It is time to monetize it.

It's time to *Monetize Your Mindset*. It's time to create a mindset that creates, in turn, continually, new streams of income – *leveraged, passive, residual income.* And enjoy a great standard of living, starting now.

It's time to become strong enough, financially, to deal with what happens, when what happens, happens.

"Success is stumbling from failure to failure with no loss of enthusiasm."

   ~ Winston Churchill

"Try not to become a man of success. Rather become a man of value."

   ~ Albert Einstein

"I can't tell you the key to success, but the key to failure it trying to please everyone."

   ~ Ed Sheeran

"Congratulations! Today is your day.
You're off to Great Places! You're off and away!"

   ~ Dr. Seuss, *Oh, The Places You'll Go!*

About the Author

He has never had a real job – and believes with his whole heart that you don't need one either (you might want one, you might enjoy having one, but you don't have to *need* one).

He graduated with a degree in accounting, a subject that he did not like and was no good at, in order to do something he would love (being an FBI agent) but did not get to do because he was automatically disqualified because of vision issues (which would not disqualify him today – except now he's too dang old to join the service).

Though discouraged and depressed, Bart moved forward. Life had given him lemons, but his father had blessed him with a monetized mindset, so he made lemonade. He soon realized he was pretty good at "making lemonade" so he built a metaphorical lemonade stand and started selling lemonade to others. He was pretty good at that too, so he became a "go to" guy for those who want to succeed when life hands *them* lemons.

His dad was a farmer, an entrepreneur; a self-made millionaire. No one would have guessed that this pig farmer (yes, Bart was raised on a pig farm) had a monetized mindset which made him wealthy. He not only instilled this same mindset into his son, he also drummed into him the importance of neighbors caring for neighbors. Helping others succeed, therefore, comes naturally to Bart Merrell.

By the way, "others" are not just "people." Bart and his wife are passionate about rescuing man's best friend – saving dogs in shelters so they are not put down. He has a Rottweiler named Diesel and a Blue Heeler/Dalmatian mix named Pebbles. He saved them both from shelters (Rottweiler is a breed often killed in shelters because they are seen as dangerous, which they aren't, not necessarily and not usually).

Today, he promotes animal rescue and he's figuring out how to monetize that too.

At nineteen, Bart left home to fulfill a two-year religious commitment in the cold northern island of Hokkaido, Japan. The people were as amazingly warm as the winters there were amazingly cold!

After returning home, he decided he liked the cold, or at least didn't hate it, and did like having four seasons instead of one (dusty), so he moved from Animas, New Mexico, to Utah State University in Northern Utah, graduating in the aforementioned accounting program with minors in Japanese and Spanish.

Today, he is an international entrepreneur, author, speaker, and training professional. He recognizes the importance of strong family ties. His "family" includes friends and neighbors both local and international. He loves helping friends help friends by building home-based businesses and other side hustles that create multiple streams of residual income.

Time and time again, Bart has proven that ordinary people can do extraordinary things just by doing ordinary things extraordinarily well.

This includes you.

Connect with Bart on Facebook at **facebook.com/bart.merrell** or at **Bart@BartMerrell.com**

About the Editor

Why would we write "about the editor"? Because he deserves our acknowledgment. Thomas Cantrell is known for his ability to hear what authors and other presenters wish to say and help them say it the way they really mean to say it. That is what a "Creative Editor" does.

His calling in life is to empower others to make the world a better place by saying the right thing at the right time, to the right people, in the right way – for the right reason. His common challenge to authors and speakers is, "go deeper."

Author and speaker in his own right, Thomas is presenter and promulgator of ideas that challenge the standard of common thought – and he gives his ideas away as fast as they come to him. He helps us get real. In quietly serving us, he epitomizes the words of Albert Pines: "What we have done for ourselves alone, dies with us. What we do for others in the world remains and is immortal."

Thomas is a creative editor, not just a copy editor or proofreader. To him, precision of meaning is ever more important than precision of spelling! If you would like his counsel on a book or a speech, call the author or you may contact him directly at:

1-801-355-2005
Tom@TomCantrell.com
AdministrativeTrialAdvocates.com